RANI DREW

PLAYS 3
Shakespeare Re-Formed

© Rani Drew, 2013,
10 Fulbrooke Road,
Cambridge CB3 9EE, UK

First Limited Edition, 2013

Acknowledgements

I would like to thank the actors of both plays for their courage to stand by the productions that challenged the Bard himself. I also thank the Romanian students who acted in *Caliban* more recently, in 2011, and Raghina Dascăl of the English Dept of the University of the West, Timisoara, for inviting me to stage *Caliban* for the opening of The First Shakespeare Symposium, Gender Aspects of Shakespeare's Work and Age.

And once again, my thanks go to my family who are the first readers and critics of my writing, a valuable asset for writers. Very special thanks to Anita once again for doing a very professional job on the technical side and John for in-setting Shakespeare's *Hamlet* into my own script and the tedious job of proof-reading.

This publication is a limited edition of 100 copies.
This copy is   /100

ISBN 978-1-871214-22-2

Contents

Off-Stage.. i

Three Plays – Shakespeare Re-Formed

The III-Act Hamlet...................... 1

Shakespeare & Me...................... 57

Caliban....................................... 109

To New Light on Old Things

Off Stage

Spring has at last arrived, late but here now. The trees are leafing and buds opening and slowly flowering, a process wonderful to watch. Just like them, I too am moving towards putting together a collection of my re-forming of Shakespeare plays. It seems a tall order to take issue with the Bard, but I can't help myself, even though it is Shakespeare Bacchi – Shakespeare Uncle - as the Hungarians call the English national dramatist and poet. They have made him their own. Shakespeare has been fully translated into Hungarian and is staged every week in at least 4 or 5 top theatres. All thespians reach their pinnacle if they perform Shakespeare Bacchi's plays and get commended.

The test is not easy. The Entrance Exam set by the Hungarian Academy of Drama is based on the acting skill of performing Shakespeare. Period. You are given three chances to prove your ability to act out the Bard's plays. I heard so many stories of these exams from passed or failed ambitious actors that it was not possible to pass up on this theme as a production plot.

I was in Budapest for eight years, teaching at one of the State Universities. The English Department supported me to set up an English Theatre Society and stage plays at the University Theatre. This resulted in my producing twelve plays not only at the University Theatre but at other theatres in the city. It surprised me that these professional theatres were happy to light up their stage for amateur plays. I suppose this was another way to open the stage doors to English theatre companies, amateurish though most were.

Here I will concentrate on my three productions which re-formed plays by Shakespeare. *The III-Act Hamlet* reframes Shakespeare's first three acts, with a series of prologues and an epilogue spoken by Ophelia's ghost. *Shakespeare & Me* takes a feminist aim at the Bard while re-weaving five female characters from different plays, *Sonnet 18*, the *'Seven Ages of Man'* speech and the song *'Come Hither'* from *As You Like It*. *Caliban* is a post-colonial sequel to Shakespeare's colonial *Tempest*. The Island comes alive after the invaders' ships sail away.

The III-Act Hamlet and *Shakespeare & Me* were performed in Budapest & then at the Annual Shakespeare Festivals in Galați, Romania (in 1992 and 1995) and won prizes. *Shakespeare & Me* won a Hungarian translation prize in 2000. In 2003, *Caliban* was given a script-in-hand production by The Blue Elephant Theatre in London. In 2011, I was invited by the University of the West in Timisoara to perform *Caliban* with Romanian students for their First Shakespeare Symposium, *Gender Aspects of Shakespeare's Work and Age*. The three plays have been Re-Formed from Shakespeare's own, in different ways.

Shakespeare's record of plays is counted as thirty six; recently I heard that he wrote four plays in the first year of his writing. A comparison with him is irresistible for me. I have written forty one plays to date, and wrote three plays in the first year of my writing, 1988; I also staged them, two in Cambridge and the third in Shanghai where I had gone to work. Not bad! I think!

Rani Drew

Play 1

The III-Act Hamlet

Right: programme of the production performed in
Budapest, Hungary on 28th, 29th, 30th May, 1992

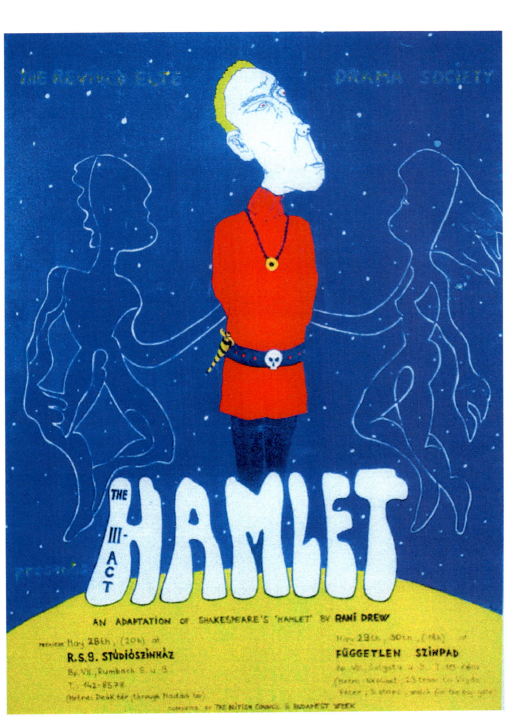

THE THREE-ACT HAMLET

Budapest, 28th, 29th & 30th May, 1992

New Prologues spoken by Ophelia's Ghost preface the first three Acts of Shakespeare's HAMLET.

STAGE MANAGER

PROLOGUE I

ACT I

PROLOGUE II

ACT II

PROLOGUE III

ACT III

EPILOGUE

STAGE MANAGER

There will be an intermission of 15 minutes.

THE REVIVED ELTE DRAMA SOCIETY

CAST

OPHELIA, CHORUS	Ariel Ducey
HAMLET	Saringer Tibor
KING	Andrew J. Nolley
QUEEN	Joann Denning
POLONIUS FRANCISCO	John Nadler
HORATIO	Martin Baker
LAERTES	Joshua Fellman
STAGE MANAGER MARCELLUS GUILDENSTERN	Rethelyi Orsi
GHOST ROSENCRANTZ	Matthew Myhrum
REYNALDO	Farkas Judit
BERNARDO VOLTEMAND	Adam Wood
PLAYERS	Johanna Wittmarschen Banyasz Bajana Schinkovits Andrea
CHILDREN	Nikowitz Kriszti Nikowitz Dorka

PRODUCTION TEAM

Stage Managers	Andrew J. Nolley Matthew Myhrum Nemeth Zsuzsanna
Music Director Flautist Drummer	Kujani Dorottya Banjasz Bajana Adam Wood
Poster Designer	Solyom Balazs
Lighting	Szabo Gyula (R.S.9) Szaloky Daniel (Fuggetlen)
Writer & Director	Rani Drew

We thank all our friends whose ready help has made this production possible.

We especially acknowledge the support of the BRITISH COUNCIL and BUDAPEST WEEK.

A Reconstruction of Shakespeare's Hamlet

The III-Act Hamlet as a feminist version of Shakespeare's *Hamlet* was premiered in Budapest, in May 1992. In an environment where feminism until very recently had no place in the popular or academic belief-system, the production did not go either unnoticed or without response. A Hungarian newspaper ran a piece with the title 'Feminista Hamlet?' questioning even a possible connection between the two words. Yet surprisingly, the response to the feminist text in the play was ground-breaking with comments such as 'You have put a new spirit into Shakespeare's ghost story', or 'A feminist perspective might at last crack the riddle surrounding the Hamlet Question'. Thus a space for the Woman Question was carved out on the Hungarian stage via Shakespeare. In writing and staging a feminist Hamlet I attempt to do more than give Shakespeare's play a different directional stance. I frame it differently, finding new boundaries from within the play, extrapolating themes and material from the text that reinforce my own interpretation.

TWO FRAMES surround Shakespeare's text: the outer frame sets a particular mood in the audience, preparing and manipulating them for the new interpretation; the second frame makes the argument in three prologues. Each prologue summarises the past, predicts the events in the following act, and thereby develops a different perspective on the original text. The interventional technique overlaps with Shakespeare's text bringing out the theme of gender that underpins the political and moral structures in Shakespeare's play.

I borrowed the device of the Prologue as a frame from Shakespeare's own play *Pericles*, and used it before each of the first 3 acts of Shakespeare's *Hamlet*.

First Frame: The Stage Manager introduces the mode, the purpose, the layout of the play along with a short history of Shakespeare's *Hamlet*. At the end, after the Epilogue by Ophelia's ghost, the Stage Manager returns and completes the frame by formally bringing the play to a close. It's possible that the innovation was prompted by the Indian classical court drama of the 7th century.

Second Frame: A technique of intervention is employed to give articulation to Ophelia's intelligence and potential which otherwise either lie dormant in Shakespeare's play or are not foregrounded. Each Prologue spoken by Ophelia's ghost as Chorus marks the development of a gender understanding in her perception as she moves from an awareness of her personal oppression to an awareness of Hamlet's.

Three Prologues

First Prologue is reconstructed with events from Shakespeare's *Hamlet*, Act IV, and precedes Shakespeare's *Hamlet*, Act I.

Second & Third Prologues lead into Shakespeare's *Hamlet*, Acts II & III.

The Epilogue summarises Shakespeare's Acts IV and V, completing the perspective on Hamlet's tragedy of resistance and failure.

N.B. In the original productions in Eastern Europe *The III-Act Hamlet* was performed with the full text of Shakespeare's Three Acts. In this printed version, for reasons of space, they have been abridged (as indicated by ellipses).

The III-Act Hamlet

Lights up. Stage Manager enters.

Stage Manager

Fifty times five thousand, perhaps, 'Hamlet'
Has been put on stage and proclaimed as
The tragedy - six deaths, to be precise
(Not counting the two off stage) -
Of a son's obsession with his father's
Murder. But there is more to Hamlet
Than mere rage over a murderous crime.
This dithering Prince of Denmark has
Successfully confused the best scholars
Of each Age. Speculations have run wild;
Questions have remained unanswered. Hamlet
Was no Hieronimo. Elizabethan savagery
Sat heavily on his enlightened mind. His
Promise to his father's ghost - you will
See presently how it's forced out of
Him - is given a long rope in the play
(Five acts, at a count). In the scheme
Of familial revenge, what was it that
Failed to convince Hamlet? 'There's the puzzle',
As Hamlet would have said. Like the proverbial
Princes, many have courted theatrical deaths
To answer the same riddle. The range is wide.
Hamlet the moralist, Hamlet the puritan,
Hamlet the misogynist, Hamlet the existentialist,
And of course, the oedipal Hamlet though he
Escapes the original tragedy of Oedipus
Marrying his mother. Tonight, this management
Makes yet one more attempt at the riddle.

The III-Act Hamlet

We bring you a feminist Hamlet. Don't get me
Wrong. There is no drama of sex change here.
The crisis of gender identity is the name of
The show this evening. Hamlet is ordered
To line up on the father's side. In fewer
Acts, extended and enlarged by our own
Text, we claim it was this imperative
That made a tragedy of his life.
                                    Lights down.

Lights go down. Flute music followed by Ophelia's song (when she is drowning) which gradually fades away. Lights come up. Chorus enters. She is dressed as Ophelia as she had looked at the time of her death. At times she uses Ophelia in the first person, at others as the third person.

Shakespeare's text follows all three Prologues.

PROLOGUE I

Chorus/ Ophelia's Ghost

Ophelia, they named her, who barely managed
To claim a patch of ground inside the sacred
Precincts. Yet for the sin of self-slaughter
She is doomed to wander the earth and atone
For the loss of her Christian will. The silence
Of after-death is peaceful, though. No songs
Of unrequited love tremble on her lips; or
Madness born of muted speech drive her to
An orgy of death. It was the deprivation
Of a protective father, and the absence
Of her betrothed to take custody of
Her orphaned self that threw her off
Balance. Like a blocked drain, long repression
Overspilled the bounds of modesty. Her coarse
Speech embarrassed the fineries of the Danish

Court. It had to come out somehow. Madness
Is the gateway to freedom. Hamlet knew that,
And she found it out, but a little too late
It was. I'm no vengeful spirit. Besides,
It's thrones and crowns that make revenge
Tragedies. Only ghosts of Kings, deposed
And murdered haunt the sons to revolt and
Claim lost kingdoms. History is full of
Righteous Fortinbras. Beheaded queens and
Heir-princesses have failed to make heroes
Of their sons. Why have I, then, returned
This night like the ghost of the Danish King?
Who could I beseech to avenge my death? Who
Bears the guilt of my self-slaughter? At
Whom should I point my dead finger? The
Father, who would not let my passion
Alone? He spied on it, regulated it
With caution, prohibition and control.

> **Polonius** (*voice over*)   This is for all: I.iii.131
> I would not, in plain terms, from this time forth
> Have you so slander any moment leisure
> As to give words or talk with the Lord Hamlet.
> Look to't, I charge you. Come your ways.   135

And Laertes, brother and playmate,
Blindfolded and bound by courtly heritage,
Was put upon to strike fear in me. Caution
And prescripts like vultures sat pecking
At my desiring heart.

> **Laertes** (*voice over*). Fear it, Ophelia, fear it, my dear   35
> Sister, and keep you in the rear of your
> Affection, out of the shot and danger of desire.
> Be wary then; best safety lies in fear.   44

Such was the brotherly love that raised in
My mind visions of cold virtue,

The III-Act Hamlet

Circumscribed and imprisoned, while
Himself remaining free and unblemished
By his own excesses. Yet, in poor
Laertes, my playmate, sorrow over my
Waterlogged body struck the human springs
So dry that no tears would flow.

And Hamlet - his neurosis o'er his mother's
Independence found me to hand - an easy
Reflection of female inconstancy.

> **Hamlet** (*voice over*) Frailty thy name is woman! -   I.ii.146
>   Within a month
>   153
> Ere yet the salt of most unrighteous tears
> Had left the flushing in her galled eyes,
> She married. O most wicked speed, to post
> With such dexterity to incestuous sheets!

Misogyny thy name is man.

> **Hamlet** (*voice over*)   Get thee to a nunnery.   III.i.122
> Why wouldst thou be a breeder of sinners?
>   141
> ...Get thee to a nunnery. Go, farewell.
> Or if thou wilt needs marry, marry a fool;
> For wise men know well enough what monsters
> You make of them. To a nunnery, go; and
> Quickly too. Farewell.

Such violence did my lord strike at me.

And the Queen, whose despair at my drowning
Spoke more of the terror hanging over
Her own womanly condition than
Compassion for my unrequited heart.

The Queen enters.

> **Queen**: There with fantastic garlands did she come   IV.vii.170

Of crowflowers, nettles, daisies, and long purples,
That liberal shepherds give a grosser name,
But our cold maids do dead men's fingers call them.
There on the pendant boughs her coronet weeds
Clambering to hang, an envious sliver broke,
When down her weedy trophies and herself
Fell in the weeping brook. Her clothes spread wide
And, mermaid-like, awhile they bore her up;
Which time she chanted snatches of old tunes,
As one incapable of her own distress,
Or like a creature native and indu'd
Unto that element; but long it could not be
Till that her garments, heavy with their drink,
Pull'd the poor wretch from her melodious lay
To muddy death. Drown'd, drown'd. (*remains on stage*)

Chorus/ Ophelia's Ghost

Drown'd, drown'd. It's no worse than when
I lived. Perhaps even better. As women,
The Queen and I were truly superfluous to the
Imperial tragedy. Moved like pawns on men's
Chequerboards - stake as high as crowns
And thrones we were, for the throw of the dice,
Polonius's two to Hamlet's two.
Codes and signs of rival systems regulated
Political rebellions and filial submissions.
For smoother operation, the terror
Must be staged early. For young saplings,
A brute show of naked power spells out the
Message clear and loud. Follow or have your
Tender genitals sliced off. Like sharp-edged
Shining sabres of treasury-guarding
Sentries, threats are flashed at the rebels.
The figure of the father appears in full
Armour. It's enough to convey the threat.
Take your place beside me, be in control of
The gender power or choose to be

The III-Act Hamlet

Less than a man. Later, no sword needs
To flash for the grown boy. Reluctance or
Doubt to fall in step with the legion is
Met with fear-striking choppers and castrated manhood.
Why and wherefore such bullying started?
Within human life there exists a state
Of equality, a gender harmony. Hamlet,
In the distant past beyond memories,
You and I were taken prisoners, pulled
Apart and enclosed in separate
Dungeons. Later, when Nature's rules
Brought our grown selves together, we
Hardly knew how firmly our worlds were
Differentiated, and set apart by
The orders of our fathers, forefathers
And a whole line of them before. It wasn't
Love that drew you to me in that first flush
Of desire. Love was lost to us a long
Time ago. So clear it's now where it
All began. Like you, Hamlet, I too have
Directed a dumb show to trace the guilt
Of a different sort of crime.

Flute music. Two children, a young boy and girl enter and run to the queen, clinging to her and kissing her. They mouth a song and rollick round her, who looks at them adoringly. Soft music is heard as they sit down as if amongst flowers, looking at each other. Suddenly, they are startled by thunderous music and the entry of the father in soldier's armour. He looks quite fierce and walks up to the mother and children, who are now huddled together in terror of his approaching figure. He takes hold of the boy, who clings to his mother's skirts, and orders him to come with him. When the boy refuses, he takes out his sword and flashes it at him. The boy covers his front in terror, shrieks and turns to the mother. The mother holds him tenderly but, looking into his eyes, implores him to follow the father. The girl takes his hand to go with him. But the father makes a prohibition sign at her. The girl looks to the mother, who also shakes her head at her. The girl and the boy are confused. The father comes closer with the sword glinting in his hand and towers over the boy threateningly. The boy appeals to the mother again, who looks helplessly at him. The boy acquiesces and lets go of the girl's hand. He follows the father, who is already leading him away, still swishing his sword noisily. Thunderous music continues as lights go down.

Chorus/ Ophelia's Ghost

Oh, that first awakening to the mother's love
Without swords and armour, without battles of
Victory and defeat. Poor Hamlet! He was
Given no choice. Nor was I. I was asked
To stay behind, he was ordered to follow. It
Was different later. In the second awakening
Of the sexual desire, of sweet love for
Another, alien to childhood memories, the
Pain of earlier separation was forgotten.
Barely was there a recognition of ourselves
As beings once equal and free. Our love had
No freedom. It was the watch word of court
Intrigues and parental matchmaking by fathers,
Brothers and uncles. Why has Ophelia,
Like the ghost of the Danish King, returned to
Haunt the play tonight? Because Hamlet and
I share the same tragedy. I am no twin of
Hamlet. But far deeper are the ties
Of intelligence, of emotion, and of
The longing for an integrated wholeness.
If our desires were the same, so were our
Frustrations with the commanding social
Strictures. In the end, we both sought
Speech through madness, and peace through
Death. Once I saw the writing on the wall,
There was nothing to stop me from using
My human will. My gains and losses were
Nil. But Hamlet, poor Hamlet, he was sucked

Into the male game of victories and defeats.
He was bound by stricter laws, unbreakable
Chains of social contracts between fathers
And sons. He wasn't keeping his side of
The deal. On that stormy night when the King's
Ghost rose on the midnight horizon, fitted
In full armour, signalling, signalling
Something, but Hamlet wasn't picking up the message.

The mother and the girl are still waiting down stage for the boy to return. When Francisco marches in and rushes past them, they leave. Bernardo follows Francisco. Ophelia watches them and then leaves.

Shakespeare's Hamlet Act I cuts in

ACT I scene i

SCENE i. Elsinore. A platform before the castle.
    FRANCISCO at his post. Enter to him BERNARDO
BERNARDO
Who's there?
FRANCISCO
Nay, answer me: stand, and unfold yourself.
BERNARDO
Long live the king!
FRANCISCO
Bernardo?
BERNARDO
He.
FRANCISCO
You come most carefully upon your hour.

BERNARDO
'Tis now struck twelve; get thee to bed, Francisco.
FRANCISCO
For this relief much thanks: 'tis bitter cold,
And I am sick at heart.
BERNARDO
Have you had quiet guard?
FRANCISCO
Not a mouse stirring.
BERNARDO
Well, good night.
If you do meet Horatio and Marcellus,
The rivals of my watch, bid them make haste....

... ...

The III-Act Hamlet

Enter MARCELLUS and HORATIO....

Exit FRANCISCO.

... ...

Enter GHOST.

MARCELLUS
Peace, break thee off; look, where it comes again!
BERNARDO
In the same figure, like the king that's dead.
MARCELLUS
Thou art a scholar; speak to it, Horatio.
BERNARDO
Looks it not like the king? mark it, Horatio.
HORATIO
Most like: it harrows me with fear and wonder.
BERNARDO
It would be spoke to.
MARCELLUS
Question it, Horatio.
HORATIO
What art thou that usurp'st this time of night,
Together with that fair and warlike form
In which the majesty of buried Denmark
Did sometimes march? by heaven I charge thee, speak!
MARCELLUS
It is offended.
BERNARDO
See, it stalks away!
HORATIO
Stay! speak, speak! I charge thee, speak!

... ...

....Exit Ghost

We do it wrong, being so majestical,
To offer it the show of violence;
For it is, as the air, invulnerable,
And our vain blows malicious mockery.
BERNARDO
It was about to speak, when the cock crew.
HORATIO
And then it started like a guilty thing
Upon a fearful summons. I have heard,
The cock, that is the trumpet to the morn,
Doth with his lofty and shrill-sounding throat
Awake the god of day; and, at his warning,
Whether in sea or fire, in earth or air,
The extravagant and erring spirit hies
To his confine: and of the truth herein
This present object made probation.
MARCELLUS
It faded on the crowing of the cock.

Some say that ever 'gainst that season comes
Wherein our Saviour's birth is celebrated,
The bird of dawning singeth all night long:
And then, they say, no spirit dares stir abroad;
The nights are wholesome; then no planets strike,
No fairy takes, nor witch hath power to charm,
So hallow'd and so gracious is the time.
HORATIO
So have I heard and do in part believe it.
But, look, the morn, in russet mantle clad,
Walks o'er the dew of yon high eastward hill:
Break we our watch up; and by my advice,
Let us impart what we have seen to-night
Unto young Hamlet; for, upon my life,
This spirit, dumb to us, will speak to him.
Do you consent we shall acquaint him with it,
As needful in our loves, fitting our duty?
MARCELLUS
Let's do't, I pray; and I this morning know
Where we shall find him most conveniently.

Exeunt.

SCENE II. A room of state in the castle.
Enter KING CLAUDIUS, QUEEN GERTRUDE, HAMLET, POLONIUS, LAERTES, VOLTIMAND, CORNELIUS, Lords, and Attendants
KING CLAUDIUS
Though yet of Hamlet our dear brother's death
The memory be green, and that it us befitted
To bear our hearts in grief and our whole kingdom
To be contracted in one brow of woe,
Yet so far hath discretion fought with nature
That we with wisest sorrow think on him,
Together with remembrance of ourselves.
Therefore our sometime sister, now our queen,
The imperial jointress to this warlike state,
Have we, as 'twere with a defeated joy,
With an auspicious and a dropping eye,
With mirth in funeral and with dirge in marriage,
In equal scale weighing delight and dole,
Taken to wife: nor have we herein barr'd
Your better wisdoms, which have freely gone
With this affair along. For all, our thanks……

....

Exeunt all but HAMLET.

HAMLET
O, that this too too solid flesh would melt
Thaw and resolve itself into a dew!
Or that the Everlasting had not fix'd
His canon 'gainst self-slaughter! O God! God!
How weary, stale, flat and unprofitable,
Seem to me all the uses of this world!
Fie on't! ah fie! 'tis an unweeded garden,
That grows to seed; things rank and gross in nature
Possess it merely. That it should come to this!
But two months dead: nay, not so much, not two:
So excellent a king; that was, to this,
Hyperion to a satyr; so loving to my mother
That he might not beteem the winds of heaven
Visit her face too roughly. Heaven and earth!
Must I remember? why, she would hang on him,
As if increase of appetite had grown
By what it fed on: and yet, within a month - Let me not think on't. Frailty, thy name is woman! -
A little month, or ere those shoes were old
With which she follow'd my poor father's body,
Like Niobe, all tears: why she, even she--
O, God! a beast, that wants discourse of reason,
Would have mourn'd longer-- married with my uncle,
My father's brother, but no more like my father
Than I to Hercules: within a month:
Ere yet the salt of most unrighteous tears
Had left the flushing in her galled eyes,
She married. O, most wicked speed, to post
With such dexterity to incestuous sheets!
It is not nor it cannot come to good:
But break, my heart; for I must hold my tongue....
....

SCENE III. A room in Polonius' house.

Enter LAERTES and OPHELIA.

LAERTES
My necessaries are embark'd: farewell:
And, sister, as the winds give benefit
And convoy is assistant, do not sleep,
But let me hear from you.
OPHELIA

Do you doubt that?
LAERTES
For Hamlet and the trifling of his favour,
Hold it a fashion and a toy in blood,
A violet in the youth of primy nature,
Forward, not permanent, sweet, not lasting,
The perfume and suppliance of a minute; No more.
OPHELIA
No more but so?
LAERTES
Think it no more;
For nature, crescent, does not grow alone
In thews and bulk, but, as this temple waxes,
The inward service of the mind and soul
Grows wide withal. Perhaps he loves you now,
And now no soil nor cautel doth besmirch
The virtue of his will: but you must fear,
His greatness weigh'd, his will is not his own;
For he himself is subject to his birth:
He may not, as unvalued persons do,
Carve for himself; for on his choice depends
The safety and health of this whole state;
And therefore must his choice be circumscribed
Unto the voice and yielding of that body
Whereof he is the head. Then if he says he loves you,
It fits your wisdom so far to believe it
As he in his particular act and place
May give his saying deed; which is no further
Than the main voice of Denmark goes withal.
Then weigh what loss your honour may sustain,
If with too credent ear you list his songs,
Or lose your heart, or your chaste treasure open
To his unmaster'd importunity.
Fear it, Ophelia, fear it, my dear sister,
And keep you in the rear of your affection,
Out of the shot and danger of desire.
The chariest maid is prodigal enough,
If she unmask her beauty to the moon:
Virtue itself 'scapes not calumnious strokes:
The canker galls the infants of the spring,
Too oft before their buttons be disclosed,
And in the morn and liquid dew of youth
Contagious blastments are most imminent.
Be wary then; best safety lies in fear:

Youth to itself rebels, though none else near.
OPHELIA
I shall the effect of this good lesson keep,
As watchman to my heart. But, good my brother,
Do not, as some ungracious pastors do,
Show me the steep and thorny way to heaven;
Whiles, like a puff'd and reckless libertine,
Himself the primrose path of dalliance treads,
And recks not his own rede.
LAERTES
O, fear me not.
I stay too long: but here my father comes………
…………

Enter POLONIUS.

…………

LAERTES
Farewell, Ophelia; and remember well
What I have said to you.
OPHELIA
'Tis in my memory lock'd,
And you yourself shall keep the key of it.

LAERTES
Farewell. *Exit*

LORD POLONIUS
What is't, Ophelia, be hath said to you?

OPHELIA
So please you, something touching the Lord Hamlet.
LORD POLONIUS
Marry, well bethought:
'Tis told me, he hath very oft of late
Given private time to you; and you yourself
Have of your audience been most free and bounteous:
If it be so, as so 'tis put on me,
And that in way of caution, I must tell you,
You do not understand yourself so clearly
As it behoves my daughter and your honour.
What is between you? Give me up the truth.
OPHELIA
He hath, my lord, of late made many tenders
Of his affection to me.
LORD POLONIUS
Affection! pooh! you speak like a green girl,
Unsifted in such perilous circumstance.
Do you believe his tenders, as you call them?
OPHELIA
I do not know, my lord, what I should think.
LORD POLONIUS
Marry, I'll teach you: think yourself a baby;
That you have ta'en these tenders for true pay,
Which are not sterling.

Tender yourself more dearly;
Or--not to crack the wind of
the poor phrase,
Running it thus--you'll tender
me a fool.
OPHELIA
My lord, he hath importuned
me with love
In honourable fashion.
LORD POLONIUS
Ay, fashion you may call it;
go to, go to.
OPHELIA
And hath given countenance
to his speech, my lord,
With almost all the holy
vows of heaven.
LORD POLONIUS
Ay, springs to catch
woodcocks. I do know,
When the blood burns, how
prodigal the soul
Lends the tongue vows: these
blazes, daughter,
Giving more light than heat,
extinct in both,
Even in their promise, as it is
a-making,
You must not take for fire.
From this time
Be somewhat scanter of your
maiden presence;
Set your entreatments at a
higher rate
Than a command to parley.
For Lord Hamlet,
Believe so much in him, that
he is young
And with a larger tether may
he walk
Than may be given you: in
few, Ophelia,
Do not believe his vows; for
they are brokers,
Not of that dye which their
investments show,
But mere implorators of
unholy suits,
Breathing like sanctified and
pious bawds,
The better to beguile. This is
for all:
I would not, in plain terms,
from this time forth,
Have you so slander any
moment leisure,
As to give words or talk with
the Lord Hamlet.
Look to't, I charge you: come
your ways.
OPHELIA
I shall obey, my lord.

Exeunt

SCENE IV. The platform.
*Enter HAMLET, HORATIO,
and MARCELLUS*
HAMLET
The air bites shrewdly; it is
very cold.
HORATIO
It is a nipping and an eager
air.
HAMLET
What hour now?
HORATIO
I think it lacks of twelve.
HAMLET
No, it is struck.
HORATIO

Indeed? I heard it not: then it draws near the season
Wherein the spirit held his wont to walk....

....

HORATIO
Look, my lord, it comes!

Enter Ghost

HAMLET
Angels and ministers of grace defend us!
Be thou a spirit of health or goblin damn'd,
Bring with thee airs from heaven or blasts from hell,
Be thy intents wicked or charitable,
Thou comest in such a questionable shape
That I will speak to thee: I'll call thee Hamlet,
King, father, royal Dane: O, answer me!
Let me not burst in ignorance; but tell
Why thy canonized bones, hearsed in death,
Have burst their cerements; why the sepulchre,
Wherein we saw thee quietly inurn'd,
Hath oped his ponderous and marble jaws,
To cast thee up again. What may this mean,
That thou, dead corse, again in complete steel
Revisit'st thus the glimpses of the moon,
Making night hideous; and we fools of nature
So horridly to shake our disposition
With thoughts beyond the reaches of our souls?
Say, why is this? wherefore? what should we do?

Ghost beckons HAMLET...

....

SCENE V. Another part of the platform.

Enter GHOST and HAMLET
HAMLET
Where wilt thou lead me? speak; I'll go no further.
Ghost
Mark me.
HAMLET
I will.
Ghost
My hour is almost come,
When I to sulphurous and tormenting flames
Must render up myself.
HAMLET
Alas, poor ghost!
Ghost
Pity me not, but lend thy serious hearing
To what I shall unfold.
HAMLET
Speak; I am bound to hear.
Ghost

So art thou to revenge, when
thou shalt hear.
HAMLET
What?
Ghost
I am thy father's spirit,
Doom'd for a certain term to
walk the night,
And for the day confined to
fast in fires,
Till the foul crimes done in
my days of nature
Are burnt and purged away.
But that I am forbid
To tell the secrets of my
prison-house,
I could a tale unfold whose
lightest word
Would harrow up thy soul,
freeze thy young blood,
Make thy two eyes, like stars,
start from their spheres,
Thy knotted and combined
locks to part
And each particular hair to
stand on end,
Like quills upon the fretful
porpentine:
But this eternal blazon must
not be
To ears of flesh and blood.
List, list, O, list!
If thou didst ever thy dear
father love--
HAMLET
O God!
Ghost
Revenge his foul and most
unnatural murder.
HAMLET
Murder!

Ghost
Murder most foul, as in the
best it is;
But this most foul, strange
and unnatural.
HAMLET
Haste me to know't, that I,
with wings as swift
As meditation or the thoughts
of love,
May sweep to my revenge.
Ghost
I find thee apt;
And duller shouldst thou be
than the fat weed
That roots itself in ease on
Lethe wharf,
Wouldst thou not stir in this.
Now, Hamlet, hear:
'Tis given out that, sleeping
in my orchard,
A serpent stung me; so the
whole ear of Denmark
Is by a forged process of my
death
Rankly abused: but know,
thou noble youth,
The serpent that did sting thy
father's life
Now wears his crown.
HAMLET
O my prophetic soul! My
uncle!
Ghost
Ay, that incestuous, that
adulterate beast,
With witchcraft of his wit,
with traitorous gifts,--
O wicked wit and gifts, that
have the power
So to seduce!--won to his

The III-Act Hamlet

shameful lust
The will of my most
seeming-virtuous queen:
O Hamlet, what a falling-off
was there!
From me, whose love was of
that dignity
That it went hand in hand
even with the vow
I made to her in marriage,
and to decline
Upon a wretch whose natural
gifts were poor
To those of mine!
But virtue, as it never will be
moved,
Though lewdness court it in a
shape of heaven,
So lust, though to a radiant
angel link'd,
Will sate itself in a celestial
bed,
And prey on garbage.
But, soft! methinks I scent
the morning air;
Brief let me be. Sleeping
within my orchard,
My custom always of the
afternoon,
Upon my secure hour thy
uncle stole,
With juice of cursed hebenon
in a vial,
And in the porches of my
ears did pour
The leperous distilment;
whose effect
Holds such an enmity with
blood of man
That swift as quicksilver it
courses through
The natural gates and alleys
of the body,
And with a sudden vigour
doth posset
And curd, like eager
droppings into milk,
The thin and wholesome
blood: so did it mine;
And a most instant tetter
bark'd about,
Most lazar-like, with vile and
loathsome crust,
All my smooth body.
Thus was I, sleeping, by a
brother's hand
Of life, of crown, of queen, at
once dispatch'd:
Cut off even in the blossoms
of my sin,
Unhousel'd, disappointed,
unanel'd,
No reckoning made, but sent
to my account
With all my imperfections on
my head:
O, horrible! O, horrible! most
horrible!
If thou hast nature in thee,
bear it not;
Let not the royal bed of
Denmark be
A couch for luxury and
damned incest.
But, howsoever thou pursuest
this act,
Taint not thy mind, nor let
thy soul contrive
Against thy mother aught:
leave her to heaven
And to those thorns that in
her bosom lodge,

To prick and sting her. Fare thee well at once!
The glow-worm shows the matin to be near,
And 'gins to pale his uneffectual fire:
Adieu, adieu! Hamlet, remember me. *Exit*
HAMLET
O all you host of heaven! O earth! what else?
And shall I couple hell? O, fie! Hold, hold, my heart;
And you, my sinews, grow not instant old,
But bear me stiffly up. Remember thee!
Ay, thou poor ghost, while memory holds a seat
In this distracted globe. Remember thee!
Yea, from the table of my memory
I'll wipe away all trivial fond records,
All saws of books, all forms, all pressures past,
That youth and observation copied there;
And thy commandment all alone shall live
Within the book and volume of my brain,
Unmix'd with baser matter: yes, by heaven!
O most pernicious woman!
O villain, villain, smiling, damned villain!
My tables,--meet it is I set it down,
That one may smile, and smile, and be a villain;
At least I'm sure it may be so in Denmark....

....

Enter **HORATIO** and **MARCELLUS**...

....

HORATIO
O day and night, but this is wondrous strange!
HAMLET
And therefore as a stranger give it welcome.
There are more things in heaven and earth, Horatio,
Than are dreamt of in your philosophy. But come;
Here, as before, never, so help you mercy,
How strange or odd soe'er I bear myself,
As I perchance hereafter shall think meet
To put an antic disposition on,
That you, at such times seeing me, never shall,
With arms encumber'd thus, or this headshake,
Or by pronouncing of some doubtful phrase,
As 'Well, well, we know,' or 'We could, an if we would,'
Or 'If we list to speak,' or 'There be, an if they might,'
Or such ambiguous giving out, to note
That you know aught of me:

this do swear,
So grace and mercy at your
most need help you, Swear.
HAMLET
Rest, rest, perturbed spirit!

*They swear. All freeze as they
touch swords in the act of
swearing.*

Chorus/Ophelia's Ghost
enters:

Living or dead, fathers hold
sons to
Filial vows sworn on swords
like real
Men. In the dark of the night,
a young
Mind is set afire with
vengeance.

Ghost
[*Beneath*] Swear.

HAMLET:
So, gentlemen,
With all my love I do
commend me to you:
And what so poor a man as
Hamlet is
May do, to express his love
and friending to you,
God willing, shall not lack.
Let us go in together;
And still your fingers on your
lips, I pray.
The time is out of joint: O
cursed spite,
That ever I was born to set it
right!
Nay, come, let's go together.

*Exeunt except Chorus/
Ophelia's Ghost*

The III-Act Hamlet

PROLOGUE II

Chorus/Ophelia's Ghost:

A daring woman, a flaunting woman must be
Avenged. Traditions must be defended.
'Be kind to your mother, Hamlet,' is mere
Gloss on the vicious revenge invoked. The
Living alone can wage wars, the spirit knows.
Theft of women is not fair game among
Men. Troy was burnt to ashes by the Mycenaean.
Helen their queen defied a long tradition.
She left the mighty Menelaus for Paris,

The prince of a pithy nation, Zeus's
Favoured city. Mere trophies of male
Warfare, neither Helen nor Gertrude were
Fit enemies worth combating. For women,
Psychological terror is enough
To subjugate, to humiliate their defiant
Spirit. The ghost of the father descends
Into the son to bring back the sinning
Mother to the fold. Would Hamlet have
Done it without the after-life melodrama?
Would anything else had deployed him from
His philosophical pursuits to bring Europe's
Dark Ages to an end? But now there was no
Escape for him. The trap was set. He was
Not the only one though. Rosencrantz and Guildenstern,
The doubting minds at Wittenberg, sharers
Of the new Renaissance spirit, and Horatio,
The trusted guide of Hamlet, all challengers
Of ageing philosophies, are seen as threats
To the old order. Fortinbras' self-exile
To the countryside rolls the drums
Of the first of many agrarian
Rebellions to come. Taxes and tithes
Are made political and landless
Peasantry banded against the rich. But
The long arm of feudal power pull'd
The defiant youth back – all to be kept
Under the cold eye of power-lusty rulers.
Observe how youth is nipped in the bud
By the 'wise reach' of the elderly.

Enter Polonius with Reynaldo downstage, instructing him. They leave.

Intrigues and conspiracies
Shadow the young like spies through the dark.
Every step towards freedom is mined with lies,
Slanders, deceit and cunning. The court is

The III-Act Hamlet

Full of the ailing and diseased, of jealous
Fathers and suspicious uncles, of spying
Statesmen and contriving Kings. The royal
Court requires tittering sycophants and
Solemn courtiers. But the young have bounded
Away. Some are in Paris, swaggering,
Sporting and drunk on unvintaged
Freedom; others remain more abstracted
In Wittenberg with sombre matters of
The mind. The spy net is thrown far and
Wide to scoop up the escaping. Youth is
Set upon youth - a caution the powerful
Take against union. Peers, pals and lovers
Are coached and trained in the art of
Surveillance. Polonius, the master politician,
Trains Reynaldo, a young lad, in the art
Of espionage - false identity, forgeries
And fake fellowship. Claudius, a superior
Statesman, more dignified and much
Sophisticated but no less prying and
Contriving, calls upon Rosencrantz
And Guildenstern to be the court
Agents and track Hamlet's stalking
Madness. No less the young Fortinbras,
Whose out-of-court rebellion is soon
Brought to heel by an 'impotent and bedrid'
Uncle-king. Such is the power of the
Elderly. Enemies or friends, battles or
Alliances, the strategy of divide and
Rule remains invariable. On which side
Are you? What's your allegiance? Which
Gender? Mother or father? Love or war?
These are not choices but threats. The
Real message is 'submit to fathers'
Rulings, or be made less manly'. The blades
Of swords glint and flash making soft flesh
Tingle with fear. Such is the dread of the
Patriarchs, the Jephthahs, the master

Hunters, the ambitious rulers and
Even the poets.

Hunters require scapegoats, chess players
Pawns and poet-dramatists actors. In this game
Of competition and combat, women and children
Become the masquerade, the prize or shame
For winners or losers. Gertrude is the
Bone of contention between the rivalling
Brothers; Ophelia, the dumb scapegoat
Strung to the tree, served as food to flush
Out the hunted beast; and the child-actors
The stage weapons of seasoned rivals to
Scale theatrical heights in the illusory
World of art. Was Hamlet's compassion for the
Exploited child actors a memory of the times
When no hunters trod woods and forests and
All was living and bounding? Gone now is
The vision of beauty and harmony.
Bloodthirsty hounds are set to hunt out the
Deep-burrowed secrets of the resisting,
Tearing them to shreds. Listen to
Hamlet's cry of kinship with the child
Actor, voice not yet cracked, imagination
So untouched that art comes to mirror life.
The dirge of the weeping Hecuba empowers
The young actor with a vision of love.
But Hamlet knows he's lost it. 'Who
Does me this, ha?' he asks in vain. Now II.ii.602
The mother is tarnished with the sin of
Whoredom, the sweetheart the stuff of brothels
Made. Is art less militant than war? It
Served the same purpose for Hamlet.
'The play's the thing', speech that breaks
The secret silence of guilty minds.

Mark, then, the players and the played,
The powerful and the weak, the old and

Young, and men against women and children -
The stuff of games, wars and art.

Enter Polonius with Reynaldo.

Shakespeare's Hamlet Act II cuts in

SCENE I. A room in POLONIUS' house.

Enter POLONIUS and REYNALDO

LORD POLONIUS: Give him this money and these notes, Reynaldo.
REYNALDO: I will, my lord.
LORD POLONIUS
You shall do marvellous wisely, good Reynaldo,
Before you visit him, to make inquire
Of his behaviour.
REYNALDO
My lord, I did intend it.
LORD POLONIUS
Marry, well said; very well said. Look you, sir,
Inquire me first what Danskers are in Paris;
And how, and who, what means, and where they keep,
What company, at what expense; and finding
By this encompassment and drift of question
That they do know my son, come you more nearer
Than your particular demands will touch it:
Take you, as 'twere, some distant knowledge of him;
As thus, 'I know his father and his friends,
And in part him': do you mark this, Reynaldo?
REYNALDO
Ay, very well, my lord.
LORD POLONIUS
'And in part him; but' you may say 'not well:
But, if't be he I mean, he's very wild;
Addicted so and so:' and there put on him
What forgeries you please; marry, none so rank
As may dishonour him; take heed of that;
But, sir, such wanton, wild and usual slips
As are companions noted and most known
To youth and liberty.
REYNALDO
As gaming, my lord.
LORD POLONIUS

Ay, or drinking, fencing, swearing, quarrelling, Drabbing: you may go so far……….
……..Exit Reynaldo

……………………

Enter OPHELIA

LORD POLONIUS
How now, Ophelia! what's the matter?
OPHELIA
O, my lord, my lord, I have been so affrighted!
LORD POLONIUS
With what, i' the name of God?
OPHELIA
My lord, as I was sewing in my closet,
Lord Hamlet, with his doublet all unbraced;
No hat upon his head; his stockings foul'd,
Ungarter'd, and down-gyved to his ancle;
Pale as his shirt; his knees knocking each other;
And with a look so piteous in purport
As if he had been loosed out of hell
To speak of horrors,--he comes before me.
LORD POLONIUS
Mad for thy love?
OPHELIA
My lord, I do not know;
But truly, I do fear it.
LORD POLONIUS
What said he?
OPHELIA
He took me by the wrist and held me hard;
Then goes he to the length of all his arm;
And, with his other hand thus o'er his brow,
He falls to such perusal of my face
As he would draw it. Long stay'd he so;
At last, a little shaking of mine arm
And thrice his head thus waving up and down,
He raised a sigh so piteous and profound
As it did seem to shatter all his bulk
And end his being: that done, he lets me go:
And, with his head over his shoulder turn'd,
He seem'd to find his way without his eyes;
For out o' doors he went without their helps,
And, to the last, bended their light on me.
LORD POLONIUS
Come, go with me: I will go seek the king
This is the very ecstasy of love,

Whose violent property fordoes itself
And leads the will to desperate undertakings
As oft as any passion under heaven
That does afflict our natures. I am sorry.
What, have you given him any hard words of late?

OPHELIA
No, my good lord, but, as you did command,
I did repel his fetters and denied
His access to me.
LORD POLONIUS
That hath made him mad.
I am sorry that with better heed and judgment
I had not quoted him: I fear'd he did but trifle,
And meant to wreck thee; but, beshrew my jealousy!
By heaven, it is as proper to our age
To cast beyond ourselves in our opinions
As it is common for the younger sort
To lack discretion. Come, go we to the king:
This must be known; which, being kept close, might move
More grief to hide than hate to utter love.

Exeunt

SCENE II. A room in the castle.
Enter KING CLAUDIUS, QUEEN GERTRUDE, ROSENCRANTZ, GUILDENSTERN, and Attendants

KING CLAUDIUS
Welcome, dear Rosencrantz and Guildenstern!
Moreover that we much did long to see you,
The need we have to use you did provoke
Our hasty sending.
Something have you heard
Of Hamlet's transformation; so call it,
Sith nor the exterior nor the inward man
Resembles that it was. What it should be,
More than his father's death, that thus hath put him
So much from the understanding of himself,
I cannot dream of: I entreat you both,
That, being of so young days brought up with him,
And sith so neighbour'd to his youth and haviour,
That you vouchsafe your rest here in our court
Some little time: so by your

companies
To draw him on to pleasures, and to gather,
So much as from occasion you may glean,
Whether aught, to us unknown, afflicts him thus,
That, open'd, lies within our remedy.

QUEEN GERTRUDE
Good gentlemen, he hath much talk'd of you;
And sure I am two men there are not living
To whom he more adheres. If it will please you
To show us so much gentry and good will
As to expend your time with us awhile,
For the supply and profit of our hope,
Your visitation shall receive such thanks
As fits a king's remembrance.
ROSENCRANTZ
Both your majesties
Might, by the sovereign power you have of us,
Put your dread pleasures more into command
Than to entreaty.
GUILDENSTERN
But we both obey,
And here give up ourselves, in the full bent
To lay our service freely at your feet,
To be commanded.
KING CLAUDIUS
Thanks, Rosencrantz and gentle Guildenstern.
QUEEN GERTRUDE
Thanks, Guildenstern and gentle Rosencrantz:
And I beseech you instantly to visit
My too much changed son.
Go, some of you,
And bring these gentlemen where Hamlet is.
GUILDENSTERN
Heavens make our presence and our practises
Pleasant and helpful to him!
QUEEN GERTRUDE
Ay, amen!.......
... ...
Enter HAMLET reading... .

Exeunt King and Queen...

... ...

GUILDENSTERN
My honoured lord!
ROSENCRANTZ
My most dear lord!
HAMLET
My excellent good friends!
How dost thou, Guildenstern? Ah, Rosencrantz! Good lads, how do ye both?................
....

ROSENCRANTZ & GUILDENSTERN
We'll wait upon you.
HAMLET
No such matter: I will not sort you with the rest of my servants, for, to speak to you like an honest man, I am most dreadfully attended. But, in the beaten way of friendship, what make you at Elsinore?
ROSENCRANTZ
To visit you, my lord; no other occasion.
HAMLET
Beggar that I am, I am even poor in thanks; but I thank you: and sure, dear friends, my thanks are too dear a halfpenny. Were you not sent for? Is it your own inclining? Is it a free visitation? Come, deal justly with me: come, come; nay, speak.
GUILDENSTERN
What should we say, my lord?
HAMLET
Why, any thing, but to the purpose. You were sent for; and there is a kind of confession in your looks which your modesties have not craft enough to colour: I know the good king and queen have sent for you.
ROSENCRANTZ
To what end, my lord?
HAMLET
That you must teach me. But let me conjure you, by the rights of our fellowship, by the consonancy of our youth, by the obligation of our ever-preserved love, and by what more dear a better proposer could charge you withal, be even and direct with me, whether you were sent for, or no?
ROSENCRANTZ
[*Aside to GUILDENSTERN*]
What say you?
HAMLET
[*Aside*] Nay, then, I have an eye of you.--If you love me, hold not off.
GUILDENSTERN
My lord, we were sent for.
HAMLET
I will tell you why; so shall my anticipation prevent your discovery, and your secrecy to the king and queen moult no feather. I have of late--but wherefore I know not--lost all my mirth, forgone all custom of exercises; and indeed it goes so heavily with my disposition that this goodly frame, the earth, seems to me a sterile promontory, this most excellent canopy, the air,

look you, this brave o'erhanging firmament, this majestical roof fretted with golden fire, why, it appears no other thing to me than a foul and pestilent congregation of vapours. What a piece of work is a man! how noble in reason! how infinite in faculty! in form and moving how express and admirable! in action how like an angel! in apprehension how like a god! the beauty of the world! the paragon of animals! And yet, to me, what is this quintessence of dust? man delights not me: no, nor woman neither, though by your smiling you seem to say so.

ROSENCRANTZ
My lord, there was no such stuff in my thoughts.

HAMLET
Why did you laugh then, when I said 'man delights not me'?

ROSENCRANTZ
To think, my lord, if you delight not in man, what lenten entertainment the players shall receive from you: we coted them on the way; and hither are they coming, to offer you service.

HAMLET
He that plays the king shall be welcome; his majesty shall have tribute of me; the adventurous knight shall use his foil and target; the lover shall not sigh gratis; the humorous man shall end his part in peace; the clown shall make those laugh whose lungs are tickled o' the sere; and the lady shall say her mind freely, or the blank verse shall halt for't. What players are they?

ROSENCRANTZ
Even those you were wont to take delight in, the tragedians of the city.

HAMLET
How chances it they travel? their residence, both in reputation and profit, was better both ways.

ROSENCRANTZ
I think their inhibition comes by the means of the late innovation.

HAMLET
Do they hold the same estimation they did when I was in the city? are they so followed?

ROSENCRANTZ
No, indeed, are they not.

HAMLET
How comes it? do they grow rusty?

ROSENCRANTZ

Nay, their endeavour keeps in the wonted pace: but there is, sir, an aery of children, little eyases, that cry out on the top of question, and are most tyrannically clapped for't: these are now the fashion, and so berattle the common stages--so they call them--that many wearing rapiers are afraid of goose-quills and dare scarce come thither.
HAMLET
What, are they children? who maintains 'em? how are they escoted? Will they pursue the quality no longer than they can sing? will they not say afterwards, if they should grow themselves to common players--as it is most like, if their means are no better--their writers do them wrong, to make them exclaim against their own succession?
ROSENCRANTZ
'Faith, there has been much to do on both sides; and the nation holds it no sin to tarre them to controversy: there was, for a while, no money bid for argument, unless the poet and the player went to cuffs in the question.

HAMLET
Is't possible?
GUILDENSTERN
O, there has been much throwing about of brains.
HAMLET
Do the boys carry it away?
ROSENCRANTZ
Ay, that they do, my lord; Hercules and his load too.
HAMLET
It is not very strange; for mine uncle is King of Denmark, and those that would make mows at him while my father lived, give twenty, forty, fifty, an hundred ducats a-piece for his picture in little. 'Sblood, there is something in this more than natural, if philosophy could find it out.

Flourish of trumpets within

GUILDENSTERN
There are the players.
HAMLET
Gentlemen, you are welcome to Elsinore. Your hands, come then: the appurtenance of welcome is fashion and ceremony: let me comply with you in this garb, lest my extent to the players, which, I tell you,

must show fairly outward,
should more appear like
entertainment than yours.
You are welcome: but my
uncle-father and aunt-mother
are deceived.
GUILDENSTERN
In what, my dear lord?
HAMLET
I am but mad north-north-
west: when the wind is
southerly I know a hawk
from a handsaw....
....

Enter **POLONIUS**
....

Enter four or five Players.

HAMLET
You are welcome, masters;
welcome, all. I am glad
to see thee well. Welcome,
good friends. O, my old
friend! thy face is valenced
since I saw thee last:
comest thou to beard me in
Denmark? What, my young
lady and mistress! By'r lady,
your ladyship is
nearer to heaven than when I
saw you last, by the
altitude of a chopine. Pray
God, your voice, like
a piece of uncurrent gold, be
not cracked within the
ring. Masters, you are all
welcome. We'll e'en
to't like French falconers, fly
at any thing we see:
we'll have a speech straight:
come, give us a taste
of your quality; come, a
passionate speech..........
....
(to **First Player**)
Dost thou hear me, old
friend; can you play the
Murder of Gonzago?
First Player
Ay, my lord.
HAMLET
We'll ha't to-morrow night.
You could, for a need,
study a speech of some dozen
or sixteen lines, which
I would set down and insert
in't, could you not?
First Player
Ay, my lord.
HAMLET
Very well. Follow that lord;
and look you mock him
not.

*Exeunt Polonius and
Players.*

My good friends, I'll leave
you till night: you are
welcome to Elsinore.
ROSENCRANTZ
Good my lord!
HAMLET
Ay, so, God be wi' ye;

Exeunt ROSENCRANTZ and GUILDENSTERN

Now I am alone.
O, what a rogue and peasant slave am I!
Is it not monstrous that this player here,
But in a fiction, in a dream of passion,
Could force his soul so to his own conceit
That from her working all his visage wann'd,
Tears in his eyes, distraction in's aspect,
A broken voice, and his whole function suiting
With forms to his conceit? and all for nothing!
For Hecuba!
What's Hecuba to him, or he to Hecuba,
That he should weep for her? What would he do,
Had he the motive and the cue for passion
That I have? He would drown the stage with tears
And cleave the general ear with horrid speech,
Make mad the guilty and appal the free,
Confound the ignorant, and amaze indeed
The very faculties of eyes and ears. Yet I,
A dull and muddy-mettled rascal, peak,
Like John-a-dreams, unpregnant of my cause,
And can say nothing; no, not for a king,
Upon whose property and most dear life
A damn'd defeat was made. Am I a coward?
Who calls me villain? breaks my pate across?
Plucks off my beard, and blows it in my face?
Tweaks me by the nose? gives me the lie i' the throat,
As deep as to the lungs? who does me this?
Ha!
'Swounds, I should take it: for it cannot be
But I am pigeon-liver'd and lack gall
To make oppression bitter, or ere this
I should have fatted all the region kites
With this slave's offal: bloody, bawdy villain!
Remorseless, treacherous, lecherous, kindless villain!
O, vengeance!
Why, what an ass am I! This is most brave,
That I, the son of a dear father murder'd,
Prompted to my revenge by heaven and hell,
Must, like a whore, unpack my heart with words,
And fall a-cursing, like a

very drab,
A scullion!
Fie upon't! foh! About, my
brain! I have heard
That guilty creatures sitting
at a play
Have by the very cunning of
the scene
Been struck so to the soul
that presently
They have proclaim'd their
malefactions;
For murder, though it have
no tongue, will speak
With most miraculous organ.
I'll have these players
Play something like the
murder of my father
Before mine uncle: I'll
observe his looks;
I'll tent him to the quick: if he
but blench,
I know my course. The spirit
that I have seen
May be the devil: and the
devil hath power
To assume a pleasing shape;
yea, and perhaps
Out of my weakness and my
melancholy,
As he is very potent with
such spirits,
Abuses me to damn me: I'll
have grounds
More relative than this: the
play 's the thing
Wherein I'll catch the
conscience of
the king. *Exit.*

The III-Act Hamlet

PROLOGUE III

Enter Chorus/Ophelia's Ghost as Hamlet is leaving.

Chorus/Ophelia's Ghost

The game of spying picks up speed. Hamlet's
Own counter-espionage is mild compared
With Polonius's human shields and Claudius's
Political conspiracy. A triangle of wits is
At work. For the renaissance man, art and
Not sword becomes the weapon - 'the play's
The thing'. It acts as it doubts. Doubt is
The first step to enlightenment. To know is

The III-Act Hamlet, Prologue I

Above: Stage Manager

Right: The Queen describes the death of Ophelia

Below: Ophelia drowned

Prologue 1 (cont.)

Above: Like Hamlet, Ophelia's ghost makes a dumb show

Right: The father's threat of castration to the boy.
Below: the father rejects the girl

Shakespeare's Hamlet, Act I

Above: Polonius chides Ophelia,
Below: the ghost tells Hamlet of his murder by The King

Above: Hamlet, "O cursed spite, that ever I was born to set it right"

Above: Laertes advises Ophelia
Below: the ghost appears again

The III-Act Hamlet, Prologue II

... tyranny on women and the exploitation of youth

Above: Polonius and Reynaldo's entry mark the end of Prologue II

Above and below, left and right: Ophelia's ghost on male vengeance, spying on the young...

Shakespeare's Hamlet, Act II

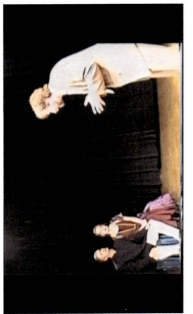

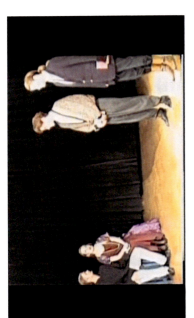

Above: Court intrigues against Hamlet
Below: Hamlet's suspicions

Shakespeare's Hamlet, Act II
Hamlet's dumb show "to catch the conscience of The King

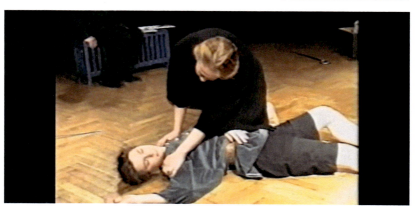

The III-Act Hamlet, Prologue III

Ophelia's ghost on court espionage, Hamlet's madness and abuse of Ophelia

Shakespeare's Hamlet, Act III

The King and Polonius eavesdropping on Hamlet and Ophelia

Shakespeare's Hamlet, Act III
Hamlet's play The Mousetrap performed at Court in front of The King

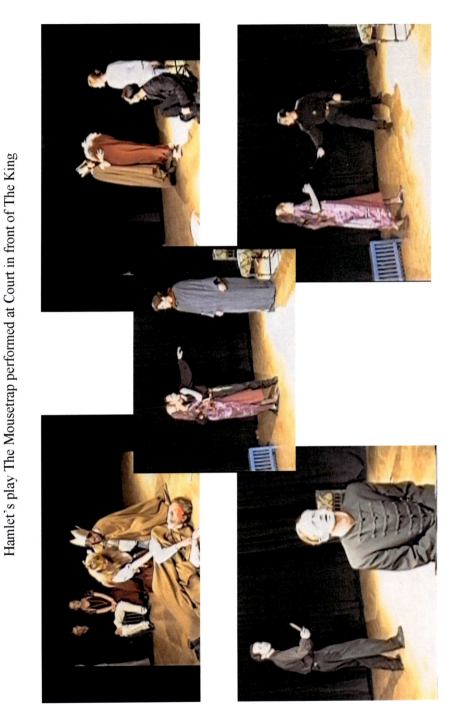

The III-Act Hamlet, Epilogue
Ophelia, Stage Manager
Director with part of the cast

The III-Act Hamlet

To doubt, doubt even the doubting mind. But
Such thinking spelled danger in feudal
Denmark. It needed a cover, a concealment,
A mediation - which Hamlet first found in
Feigned madness. But the King knew that
'Unwatched madness in great men' was a risk
Ill-afforded by politicians. Yet his own
Hard-driven espionage through Rosencrantz
And Guildenstern, gets undermined by
Polonius's medieval trust in cause
And effect motion. Did Polonius
Really believe in the power of love?
Or was it a belief in his own control?
He regulated the love between the
Young couple. Prohibitions and prescripts
Were tutors to Ophelia's desire for Hamlet.
She is told now to spurn his advances, now
To encourage his love tokens; now to
Be bold, now to be submissive. In the end,
Polonius announced that the fault lay in
His ill-timed strategy itself, which led to
Hamlet's madness. It was no honest
Admission from a statesman, a mere change
Of strategy. His faith in the sexual
Game was unshakable. So began another
Re-play of it, and I, the baby, was made
The prime spy. Like the child-actors
In theatre rivalries between poets and
'Common actors', I became the stage on
Which Hamlet and my father played out
Their stalking game. Two throws of Polonius
To two by Hamlet. Hamlet's cry against
The misuse of innocence went no further
Than reforming it to his own purposes
Of espionage. My father too coached me

In the art of speech. Hamlet's own scheme,
More artistic and moral, was no less
Exploitative. But it was he who was the
Hunted animal, much starved and on the
Run, and I the bleating goat tied in the
Clearing to flush him out for the concealed
Hunters awaiting in the bush. Sacrificial
Beast that I was in the game of the male
Hunt, it was the only time I had insight
Into Hamlet's mind. He knew what was going
On, and it terrified him. He came to see
How Love itself was used as a device to
Trap the young. Male power, male corruption,
Male distortion he saw reflected in the
Prescribed life of women. 'Get thee to a
Nunnery', the five-times repeated cry was
Not so much misogyny as a warning to women
To escape the tyranny of men. Tyrannical
Men produce weak women, who find safety
In servitude. That's how he saw his mother,
Debased by the power of men. He could see
Me going the same way. O Hamlet, why did
You lift the veil of love and see the crude
Reality? You denied me even the illusion
Of love. So be it. Something changed for
Both of us in that confrontation. All
Turned vulgar and cheap afterwards. I became
The object of sexualised violence, a mere
Masquerade for your excitable maleness. But
My failure at turning your mind inside out
Would not discourage Polonius from one
More attempt to cure your madness. He threw the
Dice again to your second throw, and claimed
Your madness was caused by a lack of
Emotional contact with your mother, a

Psychic separation from the source of
Life. Was he much wrong in that? Victimised
Find victims. You found yours in your
Mother. Watch Hamlet how he overpowers
Her, browbeats her, makes her repentant of
Her self-willed choice, extracts promises of
Sexless life, a dreary future. There was
One thing your enlightened mind failed to
Examine: what was a widow's social worth?
The ghost of your father remained over
You until you overcame your baffled mother
By your savage rage. You found your father
His peace, reinstated him in the bedroom
Of his reformed widow, relaxed in pajamas
And nightcap. But his killer still remained
At large. You failed to strike him dead, and
Your father forgot to chide you for it.
And so the revenge drama turned out to
Be a reform act exercised on the weaker sex.

Shakespeare's Hamlet Act III cuts in

SCENE i. A room in the castle.
Enter KING CLAUDIUS, QUEEN GERTRUDE, POLONIUS, OPHELIA, ROSENCRANTZ, and GUILDENSTERN
KING CLAUDIUS
And can you, by no drift of circumstance,
Get from him why he puts on this confusion,
Grating so harshly all his days of quiet
With turbulent and dangerous lunacy?
ROSENCRANTZ
He does confess he feels himself distracted;
But from what cause he will by no means speak.......
QUEEN GERTRUDE
Did you assay him?
To any pastime?
ROSENCRANTZ

Madam, it so fell out, that certain players
We o'er-raught on the way: of these we told him;
And there did seem in him a kind of joy
To hear of it: they are about the court,
And, as I think, they have already order
This night to play before him.

LORD POLONIUS
'Tis most true:
And he beseech'd me to entreat your majesties
To hear and see the matter.

KING CLAUDIUS
With all my heart; and it doth much content me
To hear him so inclined.
Good gentlemen, give him a further edge,
And drive his purpose on to these delights.

ROSENCRANTZ
We shall, my lord.

Exeunt ROSENCRANTZ and GUILDENSTERN

KING CLAUDIUS
Sweet Gertrude, leave us too;
For we have closely sent for Hamlet hither,
That he, as 'twere by accident, may here
Affront Ophelia:
Her father and myself, lawful espials,
Will so bestow ourselves
that, seeing, unseen,
We may of their encounter frankly judge,
And gather by him, as he is behaved,
If 't be the affliction of his love or no
That thus he suffers for.

QUEEN GERTRUDE
I shall obey you.
And for your part, Ophelia, I do wish
That your good beauties be the happy cause
Of Hamlet's wildness: so shall I hope your virtues
Will bring him to his wonted way again,
To both your honours.

OPHELIA
Madam, I wish it may.

Exit QUEEN GERTRUDE

LORD POLONIUS
Ophelia, walk you here.
Gracious, so please you,
We will bestow ourselves.

(To OPHELIA)

Read on this book;
That show of such an exercise may colour
Your loneliness. We are oft

to blame in this,--
'Tis too much proved--that
with devotion's visage
And pious action we do sugar o'er
the devil himself.

KING CLAUDIUS
[*Aside*] O, 'tis too true!
How smart a lash that speech
doth give my conscience!
The harlot's cheek, beautied
with plastering art,
Is not more ugly to the thing
that helps it
Than is my deed to my most
painted word:
O heavy burthen!
LORD POLONIUS
I hear him coming: let's
withdraw, my lord.

Exeunt KING CLAUDIUS and POLONIUS

Enter HAMLET
HAMLET
To be, or not to be: that is the
question:
Whether 'tis nobler in the
mind to suffer
The slings and arrows of
outrageous fortune,
Or to take arms against a sea
of troubles,
And by opposing end
them?.....

Thus conscience does make
cowards of us all;
And thus the native hue of
resolution
Is sicklied o'er with the pale
cast of thought,
And enterprises of great pith
and moment
With this regard their
currents turn awry,
And lose the name of action.--Soft you now!
The fair Ophelia! Nymph, in
thy orisons
Be all my sins remember'd.
OPHELIA
Good my lord,
How does your honour for
this many a day?
HAMLET
I humbly thank you; well,
well, well.
OPHELIA
My lord, I have
remembrances of yours,
That I have longed long to re-deliver;
I pray you, now receive them.
HAMLET
No, not I;
I never gave you aught.
OPHELIA
My honour'd lord, you know
right well you did;
And, with them, words of so
sweet breath composed
As made the things more
rich: their perfume lost,
Take these again; for to the

noble mind
Rich gifts wax poor when givers prove unkind.
There, my lord....
HAMLET
Get thee to a nunnery: why wouldst thou be a breeder of sinners?....
To a nunnery, go.

Exit

OPHELIA
O, what a noble mind is here o'erthrown!
The courtier's, soldier's, scholar's, eye, tongue, sword;
The expectancy and rose of the fair state,
The glass of fashion and the mould of form,
The observed of all observers, quite, quite down!
And I, of ladies most deject and wretched,
That suck'd the honey of his music vows,
Now see that noble and most sovereign reason,
Like sweet bells jangled, out of tune and harsh;
That unmatch'd form and feature of blown youth
Blasted with ecstasy: O, woe is me,
To have seen what I have seen, see what I see!

Exeunt

SCENE II. A hall in the castle.

Enter HAMLET and Players
HAMLET
Speak the speech, I pray you, as I pronounced it to you, trippingly on the tongue: but if you mouth it, as many of your players do, I had as lief the town-crier spoke my lines. Nor do not saw the air too much with your hand, thus, but use all gently; for in the very torrent, tempest, and, as I may say, the whirlwind of passion, you must acquire and beget a temperance that may give it smoothness. O, it offends me to the soul to hear a robustious periwig-pated fellow tear a passion to tatters, to very rags, to split the ears of the groundlings, who for the most part are capable of nothing but inexplicable dumbshows and noise: I would have such a fellow whipped for o'erdoing Termagant; it out-herods Herod: pray you, avoid it.....
....

Danish march. A flourish.
Enter KING CLAUDIUS, QUEEN GERTRUDE, POLONIUS, OPHELIA, ROSENCRANTZ,

GUILDENSTERN, and others... ... ...
... ...

HAMLET: Lady, shall I lie in your lap?

Lying down at OPHELIA's feet

... ...

Hautboys play. The dumb show enters... ... ...

HAMLET *(to Queen)*
Madam, how like you this play?
QUEEN GERTRUDE
The lady protests too much, methinks.
HAMLET
O, but she'll keep her word.
KING CLAUDIUS
Have you heard the argument? Is there no offence in 't?
HAMLET
No, no, they do but jest, poison in jest; no offence i' the world.
KING CLAUDIUS
What do you call the play?
HAMLET
The Mouse-trap. Marry, how? Tropically. This play is the image of a murder done in Vienna: Gonzago is the duke's name; his wife, Baptista: you shall see anon; 'tis a knavish piece of work: but what o' that? your majesty and we that have free souls, it touches us not: let the galled jade wince, our withers are unwrung.

Enter LUCIANUS

This is one Lucianus, nephew to the king.
OPHELIA
You are as good as a chorus, my lord.
HAMLET
I could interpret between you and your love, if I could see the puppets dallying.
OPHELIA
You are keen, my lord, you are keen.
HAMLET
It would cost you a groaning to take off my edge.
OPHELIA
Still better, and worse.
HAMLET
So you must take your husbands. Begin, murderer; pox, leave thy damnable faces, and begin. Come: 'the croaking raven doth bellow for revenge.'
LUCIANUS

Thoughts black, hands apt,
drugs fit, and time agreeing;
Confederate season, else no
creature seeing;
Thou mixture rank, of
midnight weeds collected,
With Hecate's ban thrice
blasted, thrice infected,
Thy natural magic and dire
property,
On wholesome life usurp
immediately.

*Pours the poison into the
sleeper's ears*

HAMLET
He poisons him i' the garden
for's estate. His
name's Gonzago: the story is
extant, and writ in
choice Italian: you shall see
anon how the murderer
gets the love of Gonzago's
wife.
OPHELIA
The king rises.
HAMLET
What, frighted with false fire!
QUEEN GERTRUDE
How fares my lord?
LORD POLONIUS
Give o'er the play.
KING CLAUDIUS
Give me some light: away!
All
Lights, lights, lights!

*Exeunt all but HAMLET and
HORATIO*

HAMLET
Why, let the stricken deer go
weep,
The hart ungalled play;
For some must watch, while
some must sleep:
So runs the world away.....
....

O good Horatio, I'll take the
ghost's word for a
thousand pound. Didst
perceive?
HORATIO
Very well, my lord.
HAMLET
Upon the talk of the
poisoning?
HORATIO
I did very well note him.
HAMLET
Ah, ha! Come, some music!
come, the recorders!
For if the king like not the
comedy,
Why then, belike, he likes it
not, perdy.
Come, some music!

*Re-enter ROSENCRANTZ
and GUILDENSTERN*

GUILDENSTERN
Good my lord, vouchsafe me
a word with you.

HAMLET
Sir, a whole history.
GUILDENSTERN
The king, sir,--
HAMLET
Ay, sir, what of him?
GUILDENSTERN
Is in his retirement
marvellous distempered....
The queen, your mother, in
most great affliction of
spirit, hath sent me to you....
ROSENCRANTZ
She desires to speak with you
in her closet, ere you
go to bed.
HAMLET
We shall obey, were she ten
times our mother....
....

*Re-enter Players with
recorders*

HAMLET
O, the recorders! let me see
one. To withdraw with
you:--why do you go about to
recover the wind of me,
as if you would drive me into
a toil?
GUILDENSTERN
O, my lord, if my duty be too
bold, my love is too
unmannerly.
HAMLET
I do not well understand that.
Will you play upon this pipe?
GUILDENSTERN
My lord, I cannot.
HAMLET
I pray you.
GUILDENSTERN
Believe me, I cannot.
HAMLET
I do beseech you.
GUILDENSTERN
I know no touch of it, my
lord.
HAMLET
'Tis as easy as lying: govern
these ventages with
your lingers and thumb, give
it breath with your
mouth, and it will discourse
most eloquent music.
Look you, these are the stops.
GUILDENSTERN
But these cannot I command
to any utterance of
harmony; I have not the skill.
HAMLET
Why, look you now, how
unworthy a thing you make
of me! You would play upon
me; you would seem to know
my stops; you would pluck
out the heart of my
mystery; you would sound
me from my lowest note to
the top of my compass: and
there is much music,
excellent voice, in this little
organ; yet cannot
you make it speak. 'Sblood,
do you think I am
easier to be played on than a

pipe? Call me what instrument you will, though you can fret me, yet you cannot play upon me.

Enter POLONIUS

God bless you, sir!
LORD POLONIUS
My lord, the queen would speak with you, and presently.
HAMLET
Do you see yonder cloud that's almost in shape of a camel?
LORD POLONIUS
By the mass, and 'tis like a camel, indeed.
HAMLET
Methinks it is like a weasel.
LORD POLONIUS
It is backed like a weasel.
HAMLET
Or like a whale?
LORD POLONIUS
Very like a whale.
HAMLET
Then I will come to my mother by and by. They fool me to the top of my bent. I will come by and by.
LORD POLONIUS
I will say so.
HAMLET
By and by is easily said.

Exit POLONIUS

Leave me, friends.

Exeunt all but HAMLET

Tis now the very witching time of night,
When churchyards yawn and hell itself breathes out
Contagion to this world: now could I drink hot blood,
And do such bitter business as the day
Would quake to look on. Soft! now to my mother.
O heart, lose not thy nature; let not ever
The soul of Nero enter this firm bosom:
Let me be cruel, not unnatural:
I will speak daggers to her, but use none;
My tongue and soul in this be hypocrites;
How in my words soever she be shent,
To give them seals never, my soul, consent! *Exit*

SCENE III. A room in the castle.

Enter KING CLAUDIUS, ROSENCRANTZ, and GUILDENSTERN
KING CLAUDIUS
I like him not, nor stands it safe with us
To let his madness range.

Therefore prepare you;
I your commission will
forthwith dispatch,
And he to England shall
along with you:
The terms of our estate may
not endure
Hazard so dangerous as doth
hourly grow
Out of his lunacies…..
… … … … ….

*Exeunt ROSENCRANTZ and
GUILDENSTERN*

Enter POLONIUS

LORD POLONIUS
My lord, he's going to his
mother's closet:
Behind the arras I'll convey
myself,
To hear the process; and
warrant she'll tax him home:
And, as you said, and wisely
was it said,
'Tis meet that some more
audience than a mother,
Since nature makes them
partial, should o'erhear
The speech, of vantage. Fare
you well, my liege:
I'll call upon you ere you go
to bed,
And tell you what I know.
KING CLAUDIUS
Thanks, dear my lord.

Exit POLONIUS

O, my offence is rank, it
smells to heaven;
It hath the primal eldest curse
upon't,
A brother's murder. Pray can
I not,
Though inclination be as
sharp as will:
My stronger guilt defeats my
strong intent….
O wretched state! O bosom
black as death!
O limed soul, that, struggling
to be free,
Art more engaged! Help,
angels! Make assay!
Bow, stubborn knees; and,
heart with strings of steel,
Be soft as sinews of the
newborn babe!
All may be well.

Retires and kneels

Enter HAMLET

HAMLET
Now might I do it pat, now
he is praying;
And now I'll do't. And so he
goes to heaven;
And so am I revenged. That
would be scann'd:
A villain kills my father; and
for that,
I, his sole son, do this same

villain send
To heaven.
O, this is hire and salary, not revenge.
He took my father grossly, full of bread;
With all his crimes broad blown, as flush as May;
And how his audit stands who knows save heaven?
But in our circumstance and course of thought,
'Tis heavy with him: and am I then revenged,
To take him in the purging of his soul,
When he is fit and season'd for his passage?
No!
Up, sword; and know thou a more horrid hent:
When he is drunk asleep, or in his rage,
Or in the incestuous pleasure of his bed;
At gaming, swearing, or about some act
That has no relish of salvation in't;
Then trip him, that his heels may kick at heaven,
And that his soul may be as damn'd and black
As hell, whereto it goes. My mother stays:
This physic but prolongs thy sickly days.

Exit

KING CLAUDIUS
[*Rising*] My words fly up, my thoughts remain below:
Words without thoughts never to heaven go.

Exit

SCENE IV. The Queen's closet.

Enter QUEEN GERTRUDE and POLONIUS

LORD POLONIUS
He will come straight. Look you lay home to him:
Tell him his pranks have been too broad to bear with,
And that your grace hath screen'd and stood between
Much heat and him. I'll sconce me even here.
Pray you, be round with him.
HAMLET
[*Within*] Mother, mother, mother!
QUEEN GERTRUDE
I'll warrant you,
Fear me not: withdraw, I hear him coming.

POLONIUS hides behind the arras

Enter HAMLET
HAMLET

Now, mother, what's the matter?
QUEEN GERTRUDE
Hamlet, thou hast thy father much offended.
HAMLET
Mother, you have my father much offended.
QUEEN GERTRUDE
Come, come, you answer with an idle tongue.
HAMLET
Go, go, you question with a wicked tongue.
QUEEN GERTRUDE
Why, how now, Hamlet!
HAMLET
What's the matter now?
QUEEN GERTRUDE
Have you forgot me?
HAMLET
No, by the rood, not so:
You are the queen, your husband's brother's wife;
And--would it were not so!-- you are my mother.
QUEEN GERTRUDE
Nay, then, I'll set those to you that can speak.
HAMLET
Come, come, and sit you down; you shall not budge;
You go not till I set you up a glass
Where you may see the inmost part of you.
QUEEN GERTRUDE
What wilt thou do? thou wilt not murder me?
Help, help, ho!
LORD POLONIUS
[*Behind*] What, ho! help, help, help!

HAMLET
[*Drawing*] How now! a rat? Dead, for a ducat, dead!

Makes a pass through the arras

LORD POLONIUS
[*Behind*] O, I am slain!

Falls and dies

QUEEN GERTRUDE
O me, what hast thou done?
HAMLET
Nay, I know not:
Is it the king?
QUEEN GERTRUDE
O, what a rash and bloody deed is this!
HAMLET
A bloody deed! almost as bad, good mother,
As kill a king, and marry with his brother.
QUEEN GERTRUDE
As kill a king!
HAMLET
Ay, lady, 'twas my word.

Lifts up the array and discovers POLONIUS

Thou wretched, rash, intruding fool, farewell!
I took thee for thy better: take thy fortune;
Thou find'st to be too busy is some danger.
Leave wringing of your hands: peace! sit you down,
And let me wring your heart; for so I shall,
If it be made of penetrable stuff,
If damned custom have not brass'd it so
That it is proof and bulwark against sense.

QUEEN GERTRUDE
What have I done, that thou darest wag thy tongue
In noise so rude against me?

HAMLET
Such an act
That blurs the grace and blush of modesty,
Calls virtue hypocrite, takes off the rose
From the fair forehead of an innocent love
And sets a blister there, makes marriage-vows
As false as dicers' oaths: O, such a deed
As from the body of contraction plucks
The very soul, and sweet religion makes
A rhapsody of words: heaven's face doth glow:
Yea, this solidity and compound mass,
With tristful visage, as against the doom,
Is thought-sick at the act.

QUEEN GERTRUDE
Ay me, what act,
That roars so loud, and thunders in the index?

HAMLET
Look here, upon this picture, and on this,
The counterfeit presentment of two brothers.
See, what a grace was seated on this brow;
Hyperion's curls; the front of Jove himself;
An eye like Mars, to threaten and command;
A station like the herald Mercury
New-lighted on a heaven-kissing hill;
A combination and a form indeed,
Where every god did seem to set his seal,
To give the world assurance of a man:
This was your husband. Look you now, what follows:
Here is your husband; like a mildew'd ear,
Blasting his wholesome brother. Have you eyes?
Could you on this fair

mountain leave to feed,
And batten on this moor? Ha!
have you eyes?
You cannot call it love; for at
your age
The hey-day in the blood is
tame, it's humble,
And waits upon the
judgment: and what judgment
Would step from this to
this?.............

QUEEN GERTRUDE
O Hamlet, speak no more:
Thou turn'st mine eyes into
my very soul;
And there I see such black
and grained spots
As will not leave their
tinct..........

Enter Ghost

HAMLET
Save me, and hover o'er me
with your wings,
You heavenly guards! What
would your gracious figure?
QUEEN GERTRUDE
Alas, he's mad!..........
QUEEN GERTRUDE
To whom do you speak this?
HAMLET
Do you see nothing there?
QUEEN GERTRUDE
Nothing at all; yet all that is I
see.
HAMLET
Nor did you nothing hear?

QUEEN GERTRUDE
No, nothing but ourselves.
HAMLET
Why, look you there! look,
how it steals away!
My father, in his habit as he
lived!
Look, where he goes, even
now, out at the portal!

Exit Ghost

QUEEN GERTRUDE
This the very coinage of your
brain:
This bodiless creation ecstasy
Is very cunning in.
HAMLET
Ecstasy!
My pulse, as yours, doth
temperately keep time,
And makes as healthful
music: it is not madness
That I have utter'd: bring me
to the test,
And I the matter will re-
word; which madness
Would gambol from. Mother,
for love of grace,
Lay not that mattering
unction to your soul,
That not your trespass, but
my madness speaks....
QUEEN GERTRUDE
O Hamlet, thou hast cleft my
heart in twain.
HAMLET

O, throw away the worser part of it,
And live the purer with the other half.
Good night – but go not to my uncle's bed;
Assume a virtue if you have it not...
QUEEN GERTRUDE
What shall I do?........
HAMLET
I must to England; you know that?
QUEEN GERTRUDE
Alack,
I had forgot: 'tis so concluded on.
HAMLET
There's letters seal'd: and my two schoolfellows,
Whom I will trust as I will adders fang'd,
They bear the mandate; they must sweep my way,
And marshal me to knavery....
This man shall set me packing.
I'll lug the guts into the neighbour room.
Mother, good night. Indeed this counsellor
Is now most still, most secret and most grave,
Who was in life a foolish prating knave.
Come, sir, to draw toward an end with you.
Good night, mother.

Exeunt severally; HAMLET dragging in POLONIUS

The III-Act Hamlet

EPILOGUE

Chorus/Ophelia's Ghost

The rest was not all silence. The unwitting
Murder of Polonius set Denmark
Ablaze with uncontrolled passions. There was
Ophelia's madness. Decked with flowers and
Songs, she lay down on the waters as if
On her bridal bed. Laertes, maddened by
The twin-loss, searched for the killer
And found himself leading a rising against

The III-Act Hamlet

The King. Yet impassioned youth rarely
Fathoms the subterranean reach of statecraft.
Machiavellian Claudius knew how to make
Enemy fight enemy. But Hamlet was past
The revenge cause. He wasn't interested
In Claudius's power game. He arrived to
Make his peace with the king, and slip away to
Quieter speculations at Wittenberg. Not
Even the Queen, reformed and wilting,
Drew him out of his distanced self. There
Was a short moment when my dead body forced
A burst of lamentation from him. He knew
He had traded love for obedience. Claudius
Was mistaken. The crown was never the issue
With Hamlet. It would have sat too heavily
On his head. Cornered and unadvised, Claudius
Resorted to plotting duels. Sabres poisoned
And arsenic steeped in victory toasts
Completed the scene at the Danish Court.
Four died in the end, piled on one another
Like in a collective grave. Rosencrantz and
Guildenstern suffered the worst. Their
Execution abroad must have baffled them to
The end. It was all so senseless. But for
Fortinbras it had meaning. It was his
Acquiescence to the elderly that brought
Him full reward. For the obedience to
His ailing uncle, he gave up the cause
Of the agrarian revolt; for the obedience to
Claudius, he followed correct political
Procedures; for the obedience to the State
Of Norway, he waged Polack war over a
Sterile piece of land. He obeyed all the
Powerful figures, and inherited a dual
Kingdom, much expanded and enlarged. He
And Hamlet were different men. Fortinbras,
Whose fear of the flashing sword at his

Genitals made him follow the long line of
The threatening fathers; Hamlet, whose
Doubt of the multiple image told him
It was a bogus solidarity, an empty threat.
But he was alone in that. His failure lay
In that he died for it, not lived to fight it.
Ophelia's Ghost remains on stage.

Enter the Stage Manager:

The evening now comes to an end, and
The performance over. We give our thanks for
Your patronage, and trust you'll recommend
Our efforts to your friends. We admit it
Is daring to reduce the Bard's five-act
Tragedy to three, but the reason should
Be clear by now. We have been faithful
To the tragic mode, while avoiding
Jacobean melodrama. Our perspective
Is modern. The question we felt inclined to
Explore - what was Hamlet's problem? - turned
Out to be related to our own lives.
Marching armies, pirates at sea, pools of
Blood and piles of bodies, all fell outside
The framework of our theme. We hope the
Play has yielded some thoughts to you. Born
Of living material, art must make its way
Back to reality. In this we have been
Adamant. And now on behalf of the actors,
The writer and the theatre company, we
Wish you a thoughtful journey home.

Freeze, lights go down.

The Globe Theatre, London

Play 2

Shakespeare & Me

Shakespeare the Actor, Danube Corso, Budapest, Hungary

Hungarians have made Shakespeare their own. One delightful experience is worth quoting here. As the rehearsals of the play got into full swing, I started to look for someone who could make a bust of Shakespeare for the stage. Luckily an old artist lived up the road. Since she knew no English and I little Hungarian, her daughter mediated and confirmed her mother's readiness to sculpt a golden bust of Shakespeare Bacchi (uncle), in plaster. When I went to collect it a week before the production, I found it waiting for me. There it was, a majestic golden Shakespeare Bacchi. Yet the solemn atmosphere was disconcerting. The artist was sitting with a book of Sonnets by Shakespeare in her lap, and declared that she liked reading Bacchi's sonnets to him, and could not part with him. Much as I was endeared by the artist's devotion to the Bard, I was stuck for my own purposes. I assured her I would bring him back after the performances, but she wasn't letting him leave the house. In the end, the actor who played Agnes put together a golden Shakespeare (of papier mâché) who serenely looked down from the pedestal, blessing the production in the proper Hungarian way.

FOREWORD

Set in contemporary Budapest, *Shakespeare & Me* brings together a number of present-day issues concerning women. Using Shakespeare as the axis, the play raises questions about women's secondary position in the theatre with fewer stage roles, and in real life as subordinates to men.

The dramaturgy of the play is patterned generally on Shakespeare's plays, but especially on *As You Like It*.

1) **Characters**: Agnes, the strong female character in the play, combines the strengths of both Rosalind and Celia. Eva on the other hand represents all that is averse to female intelligence and freedom in Shakespeare (the fact that women could be seen to be intelligent only if they were in male disguise), and in our own times, in present-day Hungary, despite equal opportunities under communism.

2) **Plot**: the main plot is developed in the one-hour long meeting (the length of the play) of the two friends, with the sub-plot of their relationship with their partners, Janos and Peter, who are not seen on stage. In this, unity of time and place is maintained.

3) **Techniques**: (1) the juxtaposition of tragic and comic elements highlights conflicts in relationships between characters on and off stage; Touchstone the clown and Jacques the philosopher are brought together in Agnes' view of life as an all-pervading theatre: asides and puns are used in the Elizabethan style to provide comic relief. (2) The mirror-image technique links and reflects the main plot with the sub plot in oppositional themes. (3) The theatre theme is emphasised with the use of the play-within-a-play mode.

(4) Dramatic balance is achieved through elements of change and celebration.

Multiple Critiques

1) ***Shakespeare:*** the play critiques Shakespeare's creation of female characters, who represented the male view of the female position in Elizabethan society. By rewriting the five female characters, Desdemona in *Othello*, Lady Macbeth in *Macbeth*, Portia in *The Merchant of Venice*, Katharina in *The Taming of the Shrew* and Isabella in *Measure for Measure*, *Sonnet 18* on the Immortality of Love, the *Seven Ages of Man* speech and the '*Come hither*' song from *As You Like It*, I take issue with Shakespeare's tendency to support the status quo where woman's social position was concerned, and this at a time when Elizabeth I, the strongest woman monarch, sat on the English throne!

2) ***Social Issues***: these include violence against women, anti-abortion campaign, rightwing politics and women, male-female relationship and women's fear of men. Hungarian women admit that there is a huge problem of male domination in all spheres, but are afraid to state it publicly.

3) ***Sexism & Theatre***: issue is taken with European theatre in general and Hungarian in particular, concerning questions of bias and sexism in stage productions, choice of plays and training. Recent analysis of stage roles claims that among plays generally performed there are only ten good roles for women. This highlights the fact that because there is discrimination in the selection of plays which contain great male roles it snowballs into gendered selection of applicants for the National Academy for Drama – the coveted road to success on the Hungarian stage. More females apply for admission to the Academy but fewer are selected, fewer males

apply but more are selected. The absence of women's theatre stares one in the face. And yet the general stigma of 'feminism' and its association with 'lesbianism' prevents creative women from taking a divergent course from mainstream theatre writing.

Feminist Agenda:
Adaptations & Shakespearean Stage

The play keeps to the relatively empty stage sets of the Elizabethan theatre by using a minimal stage set of a bench, a stool, a box of costumes and another of props such as masks, hats and sticks. But the most important stage set is Shakespeare himself in the form of his pedestalled statue! This has special links (1) with the Restoration, the heyday of Shakespearean adaptations, when Shakespeare was constantly brought on stage for a whole century as the ghost of the Elizabethan Theatre-Patriarch to commend or denounce the adaptations of his plays in the politicised period of post-Civil War theatre in London; and (2) with Shakespeare's first statue placed in Westminster Abbey in 1741, through the efforts of the Ladies Club formed in the late 1730s with the express purpose of restoring Shakespeare as a playwright and as a prestigious national figure; but more than that it was to enlist his support for women's writings for stage, poetry and fiction. Eliza Heywood records the contemporary scene in the *Female Spectator:*

> Some ladies indeed have shewn a truly public Spirit in rescuing the admirable, yet almost forgotten Shakespeare, from being totally sunk in oblivion:– they have generously contributed to raise a monument to his memory, and frequently honoured his works with their presence on the stage:– an action, which deserves the highest encomiums, and will be attended

with an adequate reward: since, in preserving the fame of the dead bard they add a brightness to their own, which will shine to late posterity.

Thomas Cooke, editor of the *Craftsman* hails the Countess of Shaftesbury as the supreme benefactress behind Shakespeare's canonization in 1741:

> O! Thou, whose Spirit wak'd a drowsy Age
> To pay a due Regard to Shakespeare's Page.

Shakespeare, Poets' Corner, Westminster Abbey, erected with funds raised through the efforts of the Ladies Club, formed in the late 1730s

Right: programme of the production performed in
Budapest, Hungary on November 23, 24. 26, 28, 29, 30
& Dec 2, 3, 1995

Shakespeare & Me was also performed at
The Annual Shakespeare Festival in Galaţi, Romania
in 1995, and in Cambridge in 2002.

SHAKESPEARE AND ME: THE PLOT

Set in present-day Hungary, the play is about ÁGNES and ÉVA, two young friends. ÁGNES wants to become an actor. Ever since the age of twelve she has been passionately in love with the theatre. She wants to join the National Theatre Academy - the sure way to stage success in Hungary. But she does not manage to pass the entrance exam, which in her view is very archaic and heavily loaded against female applicants. Since this is her third and last attempt she is feeling rebellious, and is prepared to do it her own way. Why not rock the boat before sinking yourself? she says, smiling.

Brought up on the cult of Shakespeare, she decides on scenes from Shakespeare as her performance piece for the exam. The required number of ten poems and five monologues, which she has prepared, are not the original writings of Shakespeare, but her own rewriting of certain scenes from the Bard's plays.

When the play opens ÁGNES is rehearsing for her entrance exam. ÉVA is helping her with the practice pieces. But ÉVA cannot stay for long as she has to get back to János, her boyfriend, who is waiting for her in a cafe.

The two friends are poles apart in their views of life. Whereas ÁGNES is independent, ambitious and broadminded with a strong self-image, ÉVA is traditional, narrow-minded and has strong opinions. As ÁGNES rehearses her speeches and ÉVA listens to her, the two come into conflict over their views on gender and politics. Their discourse on women's relationship with men reveals aspects about their lives to each other they were not aware of before. By the time the practice time is over, ÉVA is a changed person, and stays back to celebrate her new-found freedom with ÁGNES.

ELTE ENGLISH DRAMA SOCIETY
presents

SHAKESPEARE and ME

(November 23rd - December 3rd)

The action takes place in present-day Hungary.

CHARACTERS	CAST
ÁGNES (20 years)	Jane Thompson
ÉVA (20 years), a 1st year university student	Szokolyi Claudia

PRODUCTION TEAM

STAGE MANAGERS	Ujvári Erika
	Pobozsnyi Edit
PHOTOGRAPHY	F.S. Anderson
MUSIC	David Jones

WRITER/ DIRECTOR

Rani Drew

After the performance, the audience is welcome to stay and talk to the cast.

We acknowledge the support of Budapest Week and The Budapest Sun.

ÁGNES wants to be a stage actor. Shakespeare is her ideal, but she does not accept all his ideas, especially those about women. So, for her audition she rewrites eight pieces from his plays.

SHAKESPEARE	ÁGNES
SONNET 18: Power and virtue of Love	Tyranny and violence of Love
OTHELLO: Desdemona is murdered by Othello.	Desdemona wakes up in time to save herself. She leaves Othello.
AS YOU LIKE IT: Seven Ages of Man	Seven Ages of Woman
MACBETH: Lady Macbeth, the unnatural mother.	Lady Macbeth, the wife who has to give priority to Macbeth's political ambition over her own desire to be mother.
THE MERCHANT OF VENICE: Portia (as male lawyer) upholds State anti-semitism in imperial Venice.	Portia regrets fighting the law-suit against Shylock. She realises how a woman has no more rights than a Jew.
THE TAMING OF THE SHREW: Katherina, the shrew, is tamed like an animal to obey the will of her husband.	Katherina tells how denial of education by her father turns her intelligence into shrewishness.
MEASURE FOR MEASURE: Isabella, a convent novice, is waylaid by the corrupt politics of Vienna.	Isabella tells how she is first manipulated and then betrayed by the Duke. She refuses his marriage proposal.
AS YOU LIKE IT: SONG: Come hither, hither... Song of Men	Come hither, hither.... Woman (Nö*) refuses to go; Song of Women.

*Nö/nök (Hungarian) - woman/women (English)
No   - negative   (English)
Nay, Yea   - no, yes (archaic English)

Shakespeare & Me
A One-Act play

The play is about Agnes, a student (20 yrs), who wants to become an actor. Ever since the age of twelve she has been passionately in love with the theatre. She wants to join the Hungarian Academy for Drama - the sure way to stage success. But she does not manage to pass the entrance exam, which in her view is very archaic and based on gender discrimination. Since this is her third and last attempt she is feeling rebellious and is prepared to do it her own way. Why not rock the boat before sinking yourself?

Brought up on the cult of Shakespeare, an outlook particular to Hungary, she decides on scenes from Shakespeare as her performance pieces for the exam. The required number of ten poems and five monologues are not the original writings of Shakespeare but her own rewriting of certain scenes from the Bard's plays.

When the play opens Agnes is rehearsing for her theatre entrance exam. She wants to be a professional actor. It is necessary for her to train at the Hungarian Academy for Drama. All candidates are given three chances to sit for the entrance exam. This is the last time she can sit for one. She has prepared seven monologues and one sonnet as the exam pieces. These are not the original Shakespearean lines, but parodies of them. Like Hamlet, she believes in the power of the theatre. Will her delivery influence the thinking of the examiners? Will her lines shake the very foundations of the archaic power of the present stage? She is in a challenging mood. What does she stand to lose? she asks.

Her friend Eva (20 yrs), a fellow student, is helping her with rehearsing the practice pieces, but she is limited for time as she has to get back to Janos, her boyfriend, who is waiting for her in a café.

The two friends are poles apart in their views of life. Whereas Agnes is independent, ambitious, broadminded with a strong self-image, Eva is timid, traditional, narrow-minded and with hardly any sense of herself. Eva doesn't approve of many of Agnes's ways and presses her to change her attitude, especially where men are concerned. As Agnes rehearses her speeches and Eva listens to her, the two come into conflict over their political, social and religious views. Their discourse on the love and fear in women in their relationship with men, reveals aspects about their own lives to each other they were not aware of before. By the time the practice time is over, Eva is a changed person, and stays back to celebrate her new-found freedom with Agnes.

Eight pieces from Shakespeare's plays Re-Formed by Agnes

Sonnet 18

Shall I compare thee to a summer's day?
Thou art more lovely and more temperate:
Rough winds do shake the darling buds of May,
And summer's lease hath all too short a date:
Sometime too hot the eye of heaven shines,
And often is his gold complexion dimm'd;
And every fair from fair sometime declines,
By chance or nature's changing course untrimm'd;
But thy eternal summer shall not fade
Nor lose possession of that fair thou owest;
Nor shall Death brag thou wander'st in his shade,
When in eternal lines to time thou growest:
So long as men can breathe or eyes can see,
So long lives this and this gives life to thee.

Desdemona, *Othello*

The Seven Ages of Man,
As You Like It

Lady Macbeth,
Macbeth

Portia,
The Merchant of Venice

Katharina,
The Taming of the Shrew

Isabella,
Measure for Measure

Song,
"Under the Greenwood Tree",
As You Like It

Minimum lighting on stage. AGNES enters, holding a thick book in her hand – The Collected Works of William Shakespeare. *The lights go up. The room is now brightly lit, and the few things lying around in a disorderly fashion become clearly visible. Centre-stage, there is a pedestalled sculpture draped with the Hungarian flag, right side of it is a bench with a few books lying under in a haphazard manner, and downstage right-centre is a big chest stuffed with costumes and props. Next to it is a stool/chair. There is a door downstage-left which leads to the outside. AGNES is a young girl of twenty.*

As AGNES flicks through the book, reading in a low tone from the various texts, she goes round the statue in a circumambulatory fashion. She seems totally absorbed in the ritual as if she is a Greek actor, performing oblations at a Dionysian altar on stage. Soon it becomes clear that the incantations are not so reverential as the solemn low tones are followed by loud, clear comments, uttered in indignant anger. Names like Othello, Macbeth and Katharina can be heard, each time followed by phrases like 'noble murderer', 'tamed to death', and 'wronged woman', respectively. Then suddenly her eyes fall on a different page and her face lights up. She sits down on the bench, and starts reading excitedly. The lines are from As You Like It, *and are delivered loud and clear:*

> CELIA: What shall I call thee when thou art a man?
> ROSALIND: I'll have no worse a name than Jove's own page, and therefore look you call me Ganymede. But what will you be called?
> CELIA: Something that hath a reference to my state; no longer Celia but Aliena.

AGNES closes the book with a determined sound-gesture, and looks at the pedestal in a bemused way. She walks up to it and removes the Hungarian flag from it. It is a bust of Shakespeare. She places the book in front of it and gives a deep ritual bow in an Elizabethan theatrical manner. She then turns round and bows to an imaginary audience. Her movements on stage are exaggerated and stylised in the Elizabethan fashion.

'Agnes... Agnes...' is heard off stage as EVA enters in a flurry from the outside (stage-left). She is a young woman, the same age as AGNES. She looks happy, confident and full of purpose.

EVA: Good, you are in. (*Kisses her on both cheeks*). Let's get cracking. (*She looks at her watch*) I can only stay for an hour.

EVA starts to arrange the props chest, and takes the chair to stage-left, where it seems she will position herself.

AGNES: Why? You've hardly arrived.
EVA: I left Janos in a cafe. He wasn't very happy at my coming away.
AGNES: But you fixed up this time with me last week.
EVA: I know. I'm sorry. But he rang up this morning and asked me to meet him for coffee. I couldn't say no.
AGNES: Bloody man, always claiming all your time.
EVA: What's my time, if not his? And let's not waste what's ours.
AGNES: What's left of it, you mean.
EVA: (*looking at the statue*) Shall we move 'your man' further back? He seems to occupy centre-stage in your life.

AGNES and EVA move the statue back, talking at the same time.

AGNES: (*patting the statue affectionately*) At least my man doesn't throw tantrums like yours. Honestly, the way you go on about Janos this, Janos that.
EVA: What else do you expect from a woman in love?
AGNES: Passion, not emotional vacuum. You let him monopolise you totally. So, you hardly get here and you start talking about Janos as if there is nothing else in your life.
EVA: (*solemnly*) But there isn't, Agnes. And take my word for it, Janos deserves every bit of it.
AGNES: Yes, but...
EVA: (*walks up to the props chest and pulls out the trumpet, giving three sharp blows on it*) It's time for the show, my dear.
AGNES: Not yet, not yet. (*She looks for her script*) You must warn the actor first, Miss Trumpeter.
EVA: Hurry up. When's the exam, Monday or Tuesday?
AGNES: There you are! That's exactly what I mean. You call me your best friend, and you don't even remember something that's a matter of life and death to me.
EVA: I am sorry, truly. You are right. I am guilty of forgetting everyone when it comes to Janos. But that's what love does to you. Forgive me, Agnes – this once, please. (*AGNES shows no sign of relenting*). Remember: 'The quality of mercy is not strained. It droppeth as the gentle rain from heaven...'
AGNES: (*laughs*) You are wicked. You know what works on me. (*Excited*) Aren't they beautiful lines? (*Magnanimously*) Yes, I'll be merciful (*gives EVA a kiss*). Answer to your question: the exam is on Tuesday.
EVA: What time?

AGNES: 10 in the morning.
EVA: I'll be there. Do you want a last minute practice on Monday?
AGNES: Oh, yes.
EVA: (*Remembering*) No, sorry. I can't. We won't be back until late Monday evening
AGNES: Janos again? (*EVA nods her head, AGNES shakes hers*) There's no cure for your madness.
EVA: (*excitedly*) We are going to the lake on Saturday. Oh, Agnes, what bliss. If only you knew....
AGNES: No, I don't want to know, thank God. (*Loftily*) My pursuits are for something more substantial, more lasting than lovers' fantasies, which are no more than tiny bubbles of froth on the waters, blown hither thither by the first rush of winds. Here (*giving her the script*) Aliena is ready.
EVA: (*surprised*) Who's that? Someone else is coming?
AGNES: No, silly, it's me. Aliena is my stage name. In acting it helps to be someone else. It's called the stage illusion.
EVA: Very strange, this business of name and illusion.
AGNES: Don't you want to know more about the name?
EVA: All right, tell me – Aliena.
AGNES: It's the name of the best female character in Shakespeare - that splendid, wise and loving Celia alias Aliena in the Forest of Arden in *As You Like It*.
EVA: Good, it sounds good and fits you well. Let's to the stage illusion then. What are you doing first, poem or monologue? Remind me, how many are you required to learn?
AGNES: Ten poems and five monologues. Let's do a poem first. There are ten sonnets there. Pick one, that's what they do in the exam.

EVA: This is a treat, indeed. I love sonnets. All Shakespeare's?
AGNES: No, mine.
EVA: What, all of them?
AGNES: Yes, of course. Their vintage well matured for over eight years, since I was twelve.
EVA: Agnes, are you supposed to do this sort of thing? Don't you want to get into the Academy? This is suicidal.
AGNES: It won't be worse than the last two times when I recited poems of all the great writers, declaiming in our traditional (*dramatising*) style of shouting and whispering alternately, as if bouncing between two posts. Even then the great sages of the National Theatre Academy failed me. So, this time I'm going to do something different.
EVA: Making sure you'll fail this time too.
AGNES: Yes, I'll risk it. But, take it from me, one of these days those up there will have to change. (*Jumping on to the chest and, and calling out loud*) Let the National Theatre Academy look out for my genius. (*Dropping her voice*) And if I fail, at least I'll have some fun into the bargain.
EVA: (*shrugs her shoulders*) Well, it's your show, Aliena. Let's start then. What am I looking for in your type of delivery?
AGNES: Feelings, the most important part of speech. See, if the words have any effect on you; if they change your feelings, your way of looking at things. And of course, all the other aspects too, like clarity, volume, intonation etc. etc.
EVA: All right, then. (*Picks out a sheet*) Here's one. 'Love'. Ah! a theme close to my heart. Sonnet 18 re-done.

AGNES recites with great passion and humour.

LOVE

Who has not heard of you, O Love: of your
Immortal glory, your impish ways; your birth
Divine, your infantile lays. Heavens pure
Or lusty bows, you frolick so much in mirth.
Yours is the longest tale, O Child of Venus;
So many myths of birth and infancy prevail,
You never grow to manhood nor come to a close;
O Cherub round, for you there is no travail.
But enough of virtues sweet. Here I depart,
And expose the traits of a heartless foe;
Unreliable, weak-willed, merciless to a fault,
Violent and oppressive – you leave a trail of woe.
    You need reform. Forswear your plunders,
    And be on remand for juvenile blunders.

AGNES finishes with a flourish and makes a deep Elizabethan bow to EVA.

EVA: (*applauding half-heartedly*) Good, good. I like this style. It's certainly different.
AGNES: And effective?
EVA: (*hesitation*) Yes, yes. (*Quickly*) So what do we do next?
AGNES: No, Eva, I want your opinion. Out with it.
EVA: I'm here to give judgment on your skills of delivery.
AGNES: And something more I said, didn't I?
EVA: All right, then. I think you are going too far.
AGNES: In what? What the sonnet is saying or the fact that it's written by me?
EVA: Both, really. It's senselessly anarchic, and foolishly challenging. You can't afford to be either.

AGNES: Shakespeare was, and look how God-like he is to the theatre world. In this country there's even a cult of Shakespeare.

EVA: Yes, but he is Shakespeare and you are not.

AGNES: (*pointing to the sonnets*) I'm on my way to becoming him. It's not for nothing I've been kneeling at his altar since the age of five, taught by my parents to worship him like God.

EVA: Oh, such brainwashing, poor you!

AGNES: No, not poor me. I am proud of being his devotee. Now let's see; you claim to love his sonnets, but you don't know, do you, that most of them tore romantic notions to shreds? (*Reaching for the* Collected Works) I can prove it.

EVA: (*hastily looks at her watch*) No, no. You know best what you are doing, that's fine by me. I leave it to you. (*Pause*) So, let's move on.

AGNES: No, stop. There was something you were about to say, weren't you, Eva?

EVA: Oh, nothing of much importance (*starts to sort out the sheets*).

AGNES: (*taking the sheets away from EVA*) Come on, Eva. It's you this time who's wasting time.

EVA: All right. Is your sonnet saying what you really feel about love?

AGNES: (*promptly*) Yes, of course.

EVA. Is love not real? Is it all illusion and no substance?

AGNES: As testimony to my statement, listen to Shakespeare: 'Men have died from time to time, and worms have eaten them, but not for love.'

EVA: (*passionately*) Not even stuff for worms? But that's not what we are taught from the moment we are born.

AGNES: What have you been taught, Eva?

EVA: That it's the prime mover of all beings; that it's the destroyer of all ills, a power in the face of evil, a virtue against vice – I can go on forever, so endless is the list in my heart.

AGNES: What about God's love for Lucifer, his First Angel? What about God's love for Adam, the First Man, forget Eve? Didn't he throw both out of Paradise, damning them forever? Do you call that love?

EVA: What about the Virgin Mary? She is love incarnate; a spirit so selfless, so.....

AGNES: Bollocks. Poor Mary couldn't do a thing except hang her head down-

EVA: (*with a sudden burst*) What about my love for Janos?

AGNES: (*coolly*) What about it?

EVA: (*offended*) Agnes, I love him more than myself. I would do anything for him, I would lay down my life for him....

AGNES And he, what would he lay down for you, Eva? (*EVA stops short*) Is his love as selfless as yours or as Mary's? Or does he love like God – merciful yet unforgiving, spiritual yet volcanic? Its grace so exacting that if you don't 'lay down' your life for it, it burns you to cinders.

EVA: (*angry*) Is this one of your prepared speeches? You are so full of the theatre that you no longer see life. Forget it. Don't waste your precious time on the Janos-Eva story. Let's move on.

SILENCE.

AGNES: (*dramatically*)
Oh life, strike not at me for I am
Slain by Eva and can speak no more.

How does that sound?

EVA: Great. I'm glad you accept defeat.

AGNES: Slain, slain! poor Desdemona. Stung, slain
and strangled by her Lord, the Moor.
EVA: (*picking out the sheet*) So, it's Desdemona? Is it a
monologue?
AGNES: My dear Eva, wait for my magic wand. (*She throws
a shawl around her shoulders and loosens her hair*)
Hear, then, my Desdemona speaks.

*EVA settles down with the sheet. AGNES lies down,
pretending to be asleep. Suddenly she sits up, as if she
becomes aware of someone bending over her.*

    My lord, what ails thee, why look so wrathful?
    Why such anguish knits thy brow? And this
    Dagger in thy hand? Is some enemy around?

She realises something.

    What! thou meanest to kill Desdemona?
Begins to get angry.
    What manliness is this? To steal upon
    Your wife, asleep and unsuspecting of
    Your gruesome intentions? Oh, leave me
    Such gentle balm as sleep does bring
    To abused souls.

*EVA stops following the script, and looks up. She is disturbed and
seems agitated by the speech.*
    Why dost thou be
    So violent with me, Othello? You call me
    'Slut', 'whore', 'strumpet' and foul the air
    Of this chamber, love's sacred precinct;
    And yet I forgive you, seeing you anguished
    Beyond control. And now this. Should I bare
    My breast and implore you to plunge your

Soldier's dagger through? Or should I curse
The quality of my love, so whole, so trusting?
No, Othello, I shall do none of these
Any more. I shall not be sacrificed to
Your ignoble maleness. Go from me,
My lost husband, go fight the enemy
That blackened you more than your black
Colour. Alas, you heard me not sing, 'black
Is beautiful', my own love chant. Come, come,
   Othello, weep not now. The damage is done.
The fallen dagger speaks, and the clenched
Fists confirm your brutish ways more than
The slobberings of your remorse.
Though I live, your deed is done. Our paths divide,
And this my final judgment. Emilia,
Order the carriage for immediate
Departure; send a note to the governor,
Inform him of my unbending decision.
O my deluded magician, the love you once
Illumined for Desdemona is now benighted.
But I shall not sing dirges to its untimely
Death, nor say prayers for its cursed soul.
For so weak-minded proved my noble
Othello that powers craftier than his superior
Self baited him, bled him like a wild
Animal. So blind you remained to the
Blackness of souls that held you so black
That they turned the light of our lives
Into the stuff of darkness....

EVA breaks down.

EVA: (*sobbing*) Oh, stop, for heaven's sake, Agnes, stop.
AGNES: What, what's the matter, Eva? (*Holding her*) You
   are crying, you poor thing.

EVA is beside herself, her sobs get louder and more uncontrollable.

AGNES: (*theatrically, trying to humour EVA*) Such tears of boredom did my boring monologue wring from your noble heart.
EVA: Oh, for God's sake, stop this foolery. I cannot bear it any more.
AGNES: And I cannot tear it away. In truth I know not how to fare it better.
EVA: (*wiping her tears*) Stop clowning, Agnes. It has nothing to do with you.
AGNES: Who else then? (*EVA remains silent*) What? (*Shocked*) Janos? Janos an Othello?
EVA: (*bursts out crying*) Will you stop? Can't you see I am upset?
AGNES: (*getting serious*) I'll stop, if you tell me.
EVA: (*begins to speak*) It is Janos. With us it is not what it seems. He flies into such a terrible temper with me.
AGNES: Ah.
EVA: (*hastily*) You mustn't judge him, Agnes. Poor man, he's been having a lot of trouble at the office. He nearly got the boot the other day. In the end, he was let off with a severe warning to pull his weight or else.
AGNES: At least they didn't ask him to pull his socks up!
EVA: Agnes.
AGNES: Sorry, I couldn't help it. Go on. I promise I'll listen.
EVA: It's not the boss, in fact, but Szabo, his assistant, who is the real threat to Janos. Szabo is not good at his work; so last month when Janos gave him a bad report, he started to spread nasty rumours about him.
AGNES: Like what?

EVA: That Janos is often late for work; that he puts in for expenses not related to work. He even said... (*breaks down*).
AGNES: What? Go on, get it off your chest.
EVA: ...that he sexually harasses the female secretaries.
AGNES: Oh, Eva.
EVA: This is it. See, how readily you believed it. But it's not so. I know he would never look at other women Believe me, Agnes.
AGNES: I'll believe whatever you tell me.
EVA: (*continuing*) Things got pretty bad for Janos, and I ended up bearing the brunt of it. Just like me too, I failed to sense that he was having trouble at work. I just didn't see it, Agnes, (*pause*) until it all exploded like a volcano. (*Starts to cry again*) It was so sudden and so horrific. That evening when he came in, I was watching the T.V. He sat down beside me on the sofa. It was a stand-up comedy, very funny. I was laughing my head off at all the jokes. Suddenly Janos got up and left the room. I didn't take much notice of it so absorbed was I in the show. I was almost hysterical with laughter. All of a sudden as if sheets of lightning flashed around us, Janos walked in and switched off the T.V. I still didn't see it coming, and shouted out, 'What are you doing? Can't you see I'm watching it?' and got up to turn it back on. What happened next was unbelievable. (*Bursts into tears*) He turned on me like a savage beast, and before I knew I was thrown on the floor and Janos's hands were round my throat, and he was yelling, 'Bitch, slut, speak to me like that and I'll kill you.' (*Stops as she is unable to speak. AGNES waits*) I was terrified. He was growling at me. I burst into frantic cries. This infuriated him even more, and he started to bang my head on the floor again and again. I thought he was going to kill me. But the next moment he pulled me up

Above left and right: Agnes gets ready to rehearse her script.
Below: Eva arrives to help her

Above: Shakespeare's Sonnet 18 as re-written by Agnes
Below left: Desdemona (*of Othello*) wakes up and sees Othello with a dagger
Below right: the violence of Othello is mirrored in Eva's personal life

Above left and right: Shakespeare's Seven Ages of Man (*As You Like It*)
Below: Agnes's Seven Ages of Woman: mother (*left*) and ecstatic teenager (*right*)

Above left: The witches hail Lady Macbeth (of *Macbeth*)
Above right: The witches predict Lady Macbeth's guilt of Duncan's murder on her hands
Below: Eva's disagrees with Agnes's portrayal of women (*left*) and prepares to leave (*right*)

above: Agnes makes Portia (*of The Merchant of Venice*) compete and win against men
below: Agnes talks to a shrew, the tinniest creature alive on our planet (*left*) and Agnes as Kate (*of the Taming of the Shrew*), pleading with her father, not to marry her to the horse tamer (*right*)

Above: It's now Eva's turn to coach Agnes on how to be feminine

Below: Eva demonstrates to Agnes how to love a man…

… and how to nurse him

Above: Eva confesses she is frightened of Janos (*left*); Agnes tells Eva to say no to his violence (*right*)
Below: Isabella (*of Measure for Measure*) says no to the Duke's proposal (*left*); Eva now knows the word 'no', and is jubilant (*right*)

Left: Eva declares her independence

Right and below: Eva and Agnes call out to their boyfriends to join them

violently, saying, 'Stop it, get up, come to bed.' (*Beside herself*) That day was worse than death for me.

AGNES: Oh, ye gods, if you are there. (*EVA's cries get louder*) Come, come, Eva, these are too many tears. We women cry too much and make a virtue out of it. 'Dost thou think thou art virtuous' because thou makest buckets of tears? Cease to be virtuous for once, my lady in black, and be merry. Here, I'll make you laugh. Watch this.

AGNES does a mime on the 'Seven Ages of Man' speech from Shakespeare's As You Like It. *Combining the technique of a dumb show and clowning, she hams up all the roles. EVA begins to laugh. AGNES finishes with a flourish. EVA claps excitedly.*

AGNES: What was it? (*Clowning*) Answer correctly or off with your head.

EVA: (*laughing*) No chance of that, my brilliant actress. It was Jacques' speech on the Seven Ages of Man from *As You Like It*.

AGNES: (*clowning*) Correct, but here's your first lesson about the theatre, my erring theatre lover. From henceforth off with the word 'actress' for a woman. There's no gender discrimination in the word 'actor' – it's a noun and applies to all actors, male or female. So don't forget.

EVA: Nobody in Hungary will understand what you are saying.

AGNES: (*in the same manner*) Give them time, they will, bye and bye...They want to join the European Union, don't they? How now, my theatre novice, here's your second lesson of the day. Tell me what was missing in the dumb show?

EVA: (*trying to think*) Nothing, it was perfect.

AGNES: (*mocking off-with-your-head gesture*) Yes, there
was.
EVA: What?
AGNES: No woman in it. The philosopher forgot half the
human race – no woman's roles in the Seven Ages of
Man.
EVA: (*amazed*) So there isn't! You are absolutely right My
God, no Ages of Woman!
AGNES: (*continues to clown*) Forget God, he's no good
when it comes to woman. Instead, listen to my creation.

SEVEN AGES OF WOMAN

'All the world's a stage,
And all the men and women merely players;
They have their exits and their entrances,
And one 'woman in her' time plays many parts,
'Her' acts being seven ages....At first the infant,
Suckling at her mother's breast, waking at all
Hours, yelling for milk and sweet water;
The mother nodding with sleep over lusty sucks
And grabby, scratchy fingers. Then the school-girl,
Excited and bright in ribbons and frocks,
Impatient for learning, but is taught to be
A girl. In the third, there is the teenager;
The scent of blossoms in her hair, and spring
Buds on her chest. Like two tapers dreams and
Desires burn with passion in her eyes, but
Lessons of obedience and subordination,
Like snuffers put out the native glow.
The fourth age, despite all – a grown woman,
Ambitious and clever, no profession
Beyond her grasp: lawyer, engineer,
Doctor, judge and scholar – all fit like a
Glove on her slender hands, equal to any

Man. But then Cupid's arrow hits her hard,
And Hymen comes dancing in. She plays love's
Only game, loses the stake, but gains a babe.
The fifth age, Nature's own work; the wonder
Of all wonders, the body sublime. Behold the
Mother of birth and life. Her breasts like the
The swell of the sea, full and giving, never
Drying. But, a mine of creation, motherhood
And self-hood work like twins, she scales
The heights, a star bright in heaven's own
Canopy. The sixth age, she earns her rest,
Travels far and wide to see worlds myriad.
When at home, she spends long hours out in the
Garden, growing and pruning herbs and
Shrubs for the health of the young and shade
For her own calm dreams. Last scene of all,
A woman old and content; her vision
Beyond her frailty, she smiles at the
Pageant of life, though herself 'sans teeth,
Sans eyes, sans taste, sans everything.'

EVA: (*joining her in the last line, and applauding madly*)
Brilliant, wonderful. Oh, it was good to watch you! And the words, my God, you beat Shakespeare's own. They are so charged with ...with...
AGNES: With truth.
EVA: Yes, with truth. Women's truth.
AGNES: Which age did you like best? Pick one, and I'll do it again.
EVA: Motherhood.
AGNES: (*groans*) Oh, no.
EVA: Don't blame me. It's the effect of your own wonderful words for a mother.

AGNES: Well, that's art. But what about the other ages, like the professional woman who stands equal to man, and produces work just as good if not better?
EVA: Oh, God, I thought we had finished with the socialist propaganda.
AGNES: And what about motherhood propaganda? Why should that convince you more?
EVA: Because it confirms woman's natural state; she is part of nature.
AGNES: I don't want children. Am I not nature's woman?
EVA: No, you would be an unnatural woman since you'd be denying your procreative function
AGNES: I can't believe you are saying it.
EVA: But it's a biological fact.
AGNES: That a woman without a child is unnatural? That a woman's raison d'etre is her womb? It's amazing what rubbish men have stuffed into women's minds.
EVA: It's not the mind but the belly that speaks for me.
AGNES: What!
EVA: I'm pregnant.
AGNES: Whose?
EVA: Janos, you fool, who else?
AGNES: But the university? Your degree? A child and not yet twenty? Oh, you poor thing. Eva, have an abortion. It's crazy to have a child at this stage.
EVA: I can't. Janos won't agree to it. He is a born-again Christian. I would be too afraid to even mention it to him.
AGNES: But it's not his belly, for God's sake. He's not going to do a thing about it, before or after the baby is born. (*Looking at her*) You are not happy about it, Eva, are you?
EVA: (*voice heavy*) I'll miss the university life. It meant a whole world to me. And now.... my youth is passing, Agnes. I'll never be young again (*bursts out crying*).

AGNES: (*agitated*) Abortion is the only solution.
EVA: I can't. Janos will kill me. He hates women who abort the foetus. He calls them murderers, fiends and flesh-eating witches.
AGNES: Metaphors, metaphors, metaphors – the staple diet of poetry and God's truths. (*Looking at the statue*) Oh, the folly of the Bard! (*Anger rising*) Tales of witches, murderous wives and the milk of human kindness spun out to poison the childish minds of men. Come, Lady Macbeth, and show us what nature does to your sex. Right, Eva, give me a hand. Repeat after me.

AGNES dramatises Lady Macbeth and the Witches.

>*(Witches)* 'Double, double, toil and trouble,
>Fire burn and cauldron bubble.'
>Beware, beware, I smell a human;
>He approaches. Ha! a woman like us?
>Hark, her lips move. Speak, O
>Lost daughter, say what brings you here.
>Come, come....
>*(Lady Macbeth)*
>Help me, O wise women of Nature, for God's
>Scourge has fallen on the House of Macbeth.
>O you all-embracing elements, know that
>My dear husband's spirit is laden with
>Anguish so deep that it keeps him away
>From my desiring arms. No, not adultery,
>Worse than that it is. The swift-hoov'd pursuits
>Of ambition bear him away to wars
>And bloodshed. But battlefields are
>No ground for human seed; nor weapons
>The sport of love. So Time passes, and no
>Silvery Moon waxes in my dark bower;
>No ebb and flow wash up on the walls of

My womb; nor in the primordial waters
Of my being, does a human shape take root.
Oh, would that I could suckle a babe, hold
It between my warm breasts, overflowing
With nature's milk. But alas! battles
Beckon Macbeth to fields where no love
Lives. Promise to tell no one this my
Secret. Keep it between us, woman to
Woman. So, listen to me. Must I be
Handmaiden to Macbeth's bloodthirsty plan
To gain the throne of Scotland? To kill
A king! What, sweet Duncan! No, I will not hold
A dagger to a man as old as my own
Honoured father. Is this disobedience?
Will Heavens send retribution on me,
A wife who seeks her own answer, refuses
Help to her spouse? O, speak and calm the
Anguish of my heart. O Eyes of Time, give
Me intimations of what awaits this
Fated woman. O let it be the lusty
Cries of milk-yelling babes, not the fires
Of hell. O spirits benign, give me a sign
And save me from despair.
               (Witches) O Daughter
In grief, what can we do for you!
The Future is not for us to make. We
Only tell what we see. 'Double,
Double, toil and trouble, fire burn
And cauldron bubble.' Hark! asleep
Yet awake you walk through the deeps
Of the night; flickering candles
Fail to light your path, though
It's not you who's murdered sleep.
Be it as it may, O Woman cursed,
We see no child suckle at your

Bare breasts, no milk gushing out
From the nipples hard with desire.
You cry 'Water, water' to wash
The stains from hands unsoiled;
You scream for the scents of distant
Arabia to dispel the stench
Of human blood from a mind confused.

AGNES: There's a natural woman for you.

SILENCE.

EVA: (*shudders*) It's terrible to think what can happen to women and they have no one to turn to. (*Pause*) I want a daughter, Agnes. At least, there will be someone to share my troubles.
AGNES: Are you sure of that?
EVA: Absolutely. I know it. I was always there to wipe my mother's tears when things got difficult between her and my father.
AGNES: I am glad I wasn't. There would have been no end to wiping my mother's tears.
EVA: (*shocked*) You mean she needed you and you didn't comfort her? Agnes! We can't do that to our mothers. Our daughters will do the same to us.
AGNES: All the more reason for us not to be like our mothers.
EVA: What a hard-hearted daughter you are.
AGNES: It's the truth, Eva. Listen to how daughters talk about their mothers – food, care, clothes and fashion. But when it comes to work they look to their fathers.
EVA: Doesn't your mother work?
AGNES: She works in Corvina in the shoe department, hardly a model for a daughter who wants to be professional
EVA: You snob! How can you be contemptuous of women?

AGNES: In fact, it's you who has greater contempt for women. You are happy churning out the same boring functions for women from one generation to another. I'm the one who wants to break this feminine cycle.

EVA: (*nonplussed*) Women need women. I feel sorry for your mother – poor woman crushed first by her husband and then by her daughter. (*Angry*) You are a disgrace to womankind.

AGNES: What option do I have when it's mankind who butters my bread?

EVA: You get all this rubbish from Shakespeare.

AGNES: How does Shakespeare come into this?

EVA: All those motherless daughters like Cordelia and Kate and.. and even Portia, who are banished like lepers, or given away to strangers like cattle.

AGNES: I agree with you, that's why we need our own elbow grease to butter the other side of our bread.

EVA: It's all such nonsense. Put women in men's clothes when you want to get some work out of them. That's what Shakespeare does to his women; and that's what the socialists did to us. So, women are no good as women, eh? All this talk makes me sick. I think I'll leave now.

AGNES: (*stopping her*) Please, Eva, stay. You don't seem to understand me, even when I agree with you. Look, you said something about Portia. Now, she is a good example of a woman who first follows men, but then finds her own path. That's what I am saying. Do you see it now?

EVA: (*resisting*) No.

AGNES: (*Pause*) Then listen to Portia. Let her tell you how women must go beyond men. Shall I?

EVA says nothing. AGNES puts on a lawyer's cloak and collar. Reluctantly, EVA gets out the appropriate sheet and

AGNES begins.

PORTIA takes up centre-stage, as if she is in court. She has a ring in her hand.

PORTIA'S REMORSE

My work is done, and hefty gains made on
All fronts. Venice remains the champion city
Of fair law, and keeps its wide repute;
Noble Antonio released from Shylock's
Barbaric bond, breathes freely once again;
And the Duke content with his judgment
On the Jew – a punishment fair and humane.
Stripped of his last penny, Shylock is
Converted to Christian values for a
Better life here and after. His estate
Divided between the accused and his
Run-away daughter – improving prospects
For both: trade for Antonio and dowry for
Jessica. Justice is given to all
According to their deserts. For Portia?
This ring – mine own parting gift to my newly
Betrothed, Bassanio – is witness to my
Presence and performance in this Venetian
Court of men. What now, Portia, why stare
At this prize gift? Your love token, a
Promissory note for life eternal
But ha, given away to a stranger
On demand! A Christian reward for
Outwitting the shrewd Jew? No, it was
Not me, not Portia, but in disguise, a male
Counsellor from Padua. Who would believe
A woman had rid the Venetian State of a
'Currish Jew'! A seducing Judith yes,

But not a harbinger of knowledge,
Reason and law. Dare I recall the Duke
And the judges, and announce my female
Identity to a court packed with Venetian
Citizens? Would I be punished like the
Jew for flouting the Christian virtues of
Obedience and submission a woman
Must make her own? O Portia, see you now,
How like the Jew you too are ghettoed,
Your boundary marked, your inferior state
Tailor-made by men in power? Like the Jew
Your wealth is not your own, but belongs
To your husband. Fathers hand it over
Like a lottery, their daughters' fates
Locked in caskets. Can a woman stand in
Court and demand her dowry back from her
Husband, like the Jew a pound of flesh
From a defaulting borrower? O, laws so
Loaded and power so ruthless that neither
Woman nor Jew would ever receive justice.
O Portia, like a high-spirited youth, drunk
With powers so new, you pursued the Jew
Mercilessly, hounding him with sermons
Of Christian Mercy and Forgiveness. You
Would not leave Shylock the last shred of
Dignity until the Jew ceased to be
A Jew. And now I return to Belmont
To be the gracious wife who gives over
All her possessions: her wealth, her own
Ancestral seat, her virginity
To the man who won her as a lottery,
And valued her love token less than
His friendship with another man.
To Belmont then to sort matters new,
But first to the house of the Jew I must,

> Not to ask forgiveness like a Christian,
> But to own mine part in the State's crime
> Against his wealth, faith and humanity.

EVA: (*abruptly*) Yes, that was okay. (*Looking at her watch*) Hmm. There's time still, if you want to get another piece in.
AGNES: Eva, why are you like this?
EVA: Isn't it obvious, Agnes?
AGNES: No. What is it?
EVA: Well, all this rubbish of making Portia remorseful. She was absolutely right to get Shylock, as being a Jew he didn't deserve better.
AGNES: (*shocked*) Eva.
EVA: Can't you see what the Jews are doing to our country?
AGNES: What's happening to you, Eva? You never said such things before. Is this Janos again?
EVA: It is, and rightly so. Just look around, the Jews are everywhere.
AGNES: So what are you going to do?
EVA: Janos and I have joined the National Party. Hungary for Hungarians is their slogan.
AGNES: Eva, this is serious. You shouldn't follow Janos in whatever he tells you. You must think for yourself.
EVA: It's you who needs to think. You know it too well why you failed the Academy exams, and (*looking at the sheets in her hand*) little hope there is for this too.
AGNES: That's another matter.
EVA: It's not. The ones who'll get in will be the children of the new media bosses – all Jews, of course. Once the media was the monopoly of the party members, now it's the Jewish network. And you sit there doing nothing about it. I suggest you talk to Janos, join the National Party and put an end to the Jewish conspiracy in our country.

AGNES: (*stunned*) This is not you, Eva. It's Janos speaking through you. It is plain paranoia. Anti-semitism is not part of women's lives. We get nothing out of it as Portia discovers for herself.
EVA: (*getting worked up*) Oh, Portia, Portia, Portia. It's all too far-fetched. Tell me then why you don't get into the Academy? I know it, it's because of the Jews.
AGNES: (*louder*) It's nothing to do with the Jews. It's the heavy-weights sitting at the top there, bearing down on everyone with their fixed idea of what is theatre.
EVA: (*shouting more with emphasis*) They *are* the Jews.
AGNES: (*shouting her down*) Not Jews but Hungarian men whose attitude to women is the main reason.
EVA: (*deflated and confused*) I don't understand.
AGNES: The selection system is totally gendered. Fewer males apply but a greater number is taken, whereas twice as many females want to get in but fewer are admitted.
EVA: Why?
AGNES: They say because all these centuries the stage has been the domain of male writers and actors, and so all the great roles are written for men. Yet there are some plays – about ten in all – which have great roles for women, but they are never performed.
EVA: Why not?
AGNES: The excuse is that they are not so popular. But it's anybody's guess why. (*Pause*) And then there is something else, far worse.
EVA: What?
AGNES: Women are expected to sleep with men if they want to get on in their career. You know Zsuzsa, she was telling me how in the first week of her training, she got propositioned by three men, all old enough to be her father. This is how power works.

EVA: *(shocked)* That's horrible. *(Pause)* Will things ever change for women?
AGNES: They will, if women are ready to put themselves in the limelight.
EVA: How will they do it, if they can't even get into the Academy?
AGNES: They'll have to do it outside the Academy then. They will have to start a new type of theatre and write about themselves. Do you know, there is not one woman in this country who writes about women from a woman's point of view?
EVA: Well, this is where we go our different ways. And I say thank God there are not too many Alienas in our country, filling the sky with the sound of 'women, women, women'.
AGNES: Wouldn't that be good – for a change?
EVA: *(serious)* It's dangerous, Agnes, for women to go on about themselves. It puts men off. They don't want to hear about it the whole time. No wonder you don't have a boyfriend.
AGNES: Thanks for that dig. And how do you know I don't?
EVA: You've never mentioned anyone. Also, I know for certain, men can't cope with headstrong women.
AGNES: You think *(dramatically)* I am monstrously headstrong and uncontrollably shrewish?
EVA: O, certainly.
AGNES: A gone case or tameable?
EVA: Oh, no. All women can be tamed. *(Giving her a close look)* Now let me see about you. Hmm, I think a few tips on how to be feminine would make a new woman out of you.
AGNES: You reckon?
EVA: Yes, I can prove it now.
AGNES: On one condition.
EVA: What's that?

AGNES: First you listen to what my shrew has to say after she's been tamed.
EVA: A deal. You'll have to be short, though. I should be going soon.
AGNES: (*clowning*) The Shrew will be quick about her tameness.

KATE THE SHREW

The case of a shrew is a case for all.
So, listen with thought and give as fair
A judgment as you want for yourself. A shrew,
Mammalogy informs us, is the tiniest
Creature alive on our planet. A venomous,
Deadly insect, a carrier of death
To animals many times larger and heftier
Than its own mean size. Should it refute
Claims superior, savage attacks are made
On its existence. A woman is a shrew,
They say, who behaves like the shrew.
Ah, Katherina, as the first born
Of a wealthy Italian, you knew very early
That a woman can be made a fool by men,
Unless she resists. Grown in the sunlight
Of my father's ways of domination
And authority, I had no education,
No knowledge of the arts or the sciences,
A domain of men alone. No wonder
My talents became unruly, the energy
Wayward. Across the field of memories,
No softer images of a mother beckoned,
No recollection of loving eyes lit
The path to the times I suckled her breasts;
Nor sounds of gentle lullabies filled
My little mind with lessons of female

Submission to her lord and master. Quick
To imitate my father's mien I was swift to
Practise on Bianca, my younger sister,
Sly and a weepy tell-tale of my hot
Temper. But she had her feminine revenge,
When suitors lined up before my father.
Whereas the news of her virtues brought
Many to her marriage stalls, mine were down
To nil. Good news it was for me, but to my
Father a source of worry it became.
But then arrived the master of a taming
School whose skill of taming wild animals
Challenged him to try it on free women;
A tough bargainer, he asked my father
For coins in gold, a compensation for
My less mild nature, and a free hand to 'woo,
Wed and bed' his daughter wild. O father,
I pleaded, marry me not to this tamer,
A man cruel; his eyes are dungeons dark,
No sign of light or air within. Keep me
A slave in your house, if a slave I have
To be.
      Oh fates cruel that make a woman
Helpless in men's transactions. Petruchio,
The master tamer, marched me off like an
Animal bought. So be it, I said, and
Prepared myself for the worst. I knew men
Make fools of women who fail to resist;
I answered his ruthless ways with open
Defiance. But abandoned by a father and
No mother to turn to, I soon gave up
The struggle. Like a beast I was starv'd,
Baited and stripped of dignity. Now look
At me, a shrew tamed, broken in like a colt,
Timid, fearing and obedient to the tamer,

> I echo the will and whim of my master.

AGNES looks at EVA. Silence.

EVA: A truly horrible story, but it proves my point. Why put yourself in fathers' or husbands' hands when your mother or mother-like women (*pointing to herself*) can do the job with care and compassion?
AGNES: The result is just as bad. We are prepared for men, period.
EVA: Ah, but there's a difference. When men reform women they take the sting out of them. When women do it to women they make them more powerful.
AGNES: It doesn't convince me.
EVA: Let me show you then; give me fifteen minutes. Sit down on this bench here. Right. You are a man, and I'm your girl-friend. Now, you act whatever type of man you want to: tough, impossible, unreasonable, macho, cruel, abusive – whatever, and I'll deal with you. Okay?
AGNES: Okay. But how is it going to tame my shrewishness?
EVA: Sshh. Just wait. It's a different approach.

AGNES sits down, EVA goes to the outer-door exit, and then pretends to enter the room.

> Hi.....stop. What's your boyfriend's name?

AGNES: Peter.
EVA: Hm. Peter, I like the name. And I am, of course, Agnes.
AGNES: And I am Peter.
EVA: Okay, start again. Hi, Peter.
AGNES/PETER: (*grunts*) Hi…
EVA/AGNES: What's the matter, honey? Is something wrong, my love?

AGNES: Aren't you overdoing it, Eva, with all this love business? He's not God, after all.
EVA: (*remonstrating*) That's the problem with you, Agnes. You question the ego of men too much. Of course, they believe they are God. And they've good reason since it's them who thought of God.
AGNES: Too bad. I'm not going to pander to any God – fake or real.
EVA: We'll see. Shall we get back to our session? Now, no interruptions this time.

AGNES goes back to being PETER. EVA as AGNES comes over and puts her arms round her. The asides in their speeches are sometimes part of the play-making, sometimes their own comments on the role-play.

What's the matter, darling? Are you in a mood? Have I said something that annoyed you?
AGNES/PETER: (*aside*) Like hell, darling – I have a headache.
EVA/AGNES: (*aside:* Fake excuse) How awful. (*Presses his temples*) Let me send your headache away. (*Continues*) Is it getting better, darling? *(AGNES/PETER doesn't bother to reply and acts moodily).* Aren't you going to say something? (*He doesn't*) Shall I cook some food?
AGNES/PETER: (*perks up*) Yes.
EVA/AGNES: Perhaps you'll talk then?
AGNES/PETER: About what?
EVA/AGNES: Why you are in a mood.
AGNES/PETER: Am I? What are we eating?
EVA/AGNES: What do you want? Goulash or palacsintas?
AGNES/PETER: (*brightening up*) Palacsintas?
EVA/AGNES: Savoury or sweet?

AGNES/PETER: (*aside*) Not on my life, but carry on – with dios and chocolate sauce. Thank you, Agnes. You are such an angel.

EVA smiles sweetly and proceeds to the kitchen (inner exit).

EVA/AGNES: (*looking around, aside:* Strategy no. 2). Darling, the place is in a mess. (*Scolding*) You really ought to be a bit more tidy, Peter. (*Obligingly*) Do you want me to clean the place? (*Aside:* This will impress on him my usefulness).
AGNES/PETER: (*aside:* Never, on my life) That's sweet of you, Agnes. Life would be a total mess without you.
EVA/AGNES: (*aside:* This is the time to strike, the iron is hot). Peter I want to talk to you about something.
AGNES/PETER: (*without looking up*) What?
EVA/AGNES (*aside:* This is called 'moving into marriage' strategy). You know, sometimes I get tired of these comings and goings. (*Putting her arms round him*) I mean, when I come here I don't want to go away from you.
AGNES/PETER: (*yawns*) You don't? Why not?
EVA/AGNES: Because (*aside:* You blockhead) I love you and want to be with you forever and forever.
AGNES/PETER: (*aside:* I have to watch this). But then I won't be able to read my books. You always want to talk.
EVA/AGNES: Of course (*aside*: I'll get him soon). Isn't that what people in love do? Tell each other little things, whisper sweet nothings. (*Aside:* Quick, change tack). I think we should get married.
AGNES/PETER: (*first time looks at her*) What? I didn't think you were interested in marriage. And I am not sure if you are the right person for me.

EVA: (*gobsmacked*) How dare he, Agnes! Is that what Peter says? (*AGNES nods her* head). And you, you want marriage?
AGNES: Maybe eventually. But right now, I want him to take me more seriously.
EVA: In what way?
AGNES: I want him to be more active in our relationship. At present. he is literally a..a blob. (*They stand looking at each other*).
EVA: Hmm. All right then. The situation demands what is called the 'trump feminine' strategy. Watch me now. (*In a firm voice*) Peter, it can't go on like this. You have to make up your mind.
AGNES/PETER: (*surprised*) About what?
EVA/AGNES: (*shouting*) About our marriage, man/
AGNES: (*interrupting*) No, not marriage I said, Eva.
EVA: I have to say marriage, Agnes. Just wait.
AGNES: As long as you know what I really want.
EVA/AGNES: (*resuming*) I shall not go on with this arrangement.
AGNES/PETER: Why not, what's the matter with you today?
EVA/AGNES: (*shouting louder*) No more, do you understand me? I come here, cook for you, clean your flat/...
AGNES: (*protesting*) But I don't, Eva.
EVA: Don't interrupt, Agnes. (*Continuing as PETER*) / sleep with you and then clear out. It's worse than slavery. It's got to stop, Peter. Take it or leave it – and I mean it this time.
AGNES: (*stopping*) No, Eva. I'd never want to get him through ultimatums.
EVA: (*giving up*) So what do you want?
AGNES: Look, what I want is a lively relationship in which both of us participate. I don't want to be his cleaning lady or the cook or the nurse; damn it, I want a partner,

not a patient. So give me another solution, not forced marriage.

EVA: Not marriage! (*Thinks*) Tell me more about him then.

AGNES: You know there are two types of men these days. One is the traditional type – like Janos – who says: I'll love you and dump you/

EVA: What's that?

AGNES: I'll marry you, if you do as I say.

EVA: Okay, yes. I know that one.

AGNES: So he tells you what to do, what to think, where to go, how to speak; where to sit, where to stand, in short he domesticates you.

EVA: (*amazed*) How do you know all this? This is how it is with us. Janos works out every small detail of our lives. You know why I go to my mother for two days in the week?

AGNES: Because you want to see your mother?

EVA: No, because Janos wants to be alone.

AGNES: Something arranged by the calendar?

EVA: Yes, it's a weekly system. I return to my mother's on Tuesday, stay with her on Wednesday, and come back to Janos on Thursday.

AGNES: And all this because he can't bear your presence seven days a week?

EVA: That's it.

AGNES: Why do you put up with it, Eva?

EVA: It's love, Agnes. As long as I am in love with Janos, I'll do whatever he wants me to. But I feel sorry for my mother.

AGNES: I would. Poor woman.

EVA: As it is, she didn't approve of my setting up with Janos, but then to see her daughter sent home every week is even more humiliating for her.

AGNES: Like a dog sent to the kennels when the master goes on holiday! I don't understand why you let him manipulate you.
EVA: Because men like to manage women. And if the women don't let them, they won't have them.

AGNES looks at EVA. Both remain silent.

   (*Breaks the silence*) What about the second type of man?
AGNES: Well, he is the new man like Peter: liberal, intelligent and accepting. But sadly he is not much better. He says, 'I leave everything to you. Do whatever you like.'
EVA: (*contemptuously*) Sounds like a henpecked husband.
AGNES: No, he is not henpecked. He simply ceases to operate, to take any initiative himself. So the woman ends up taking care of everything: she initiates conversations, suggests outings or holidays, makes arrangements, pays for the fare, remembers all the dates; she decides on which friends to make, which to keep, which to drop etc. etc. In a nutshell, for their personal, social and emotional life she has a sleeping partner.
EVA: Sounds like a regular married life to me. (*Sighing*) Well, Agnes, between the two of us, we've rounded up all that is available, and neither of us is better off. You are free – and don't want to be particularly free; and I am not free at all – and don't care about it. (*They look at each other*). What is to be done?

PAUSE

AGNES: We must assert our wills.
EVA: With or without a man.

AGNES: You with Janos, a macho man; and I with Peter, a liberal man.
EVA: Tell me how?
AGNES: It won't be easy. I have to think.

AGNES paces the stage. EVA looks at AGNES from time to time, expecting her to come up with an answer.

Something can be done, (*looking at EVA seriously*) but it means we have to work together.
EVA: (*alarmed*) What, I have to agree with you?
AGNES: Not entirely, but we have to join forces.
EVA: (*suspiciously*) What does that mean? It sounds risky.
AGNES: Relax. It's not going to be a revolution. Just a confrontation – an honest and simple self-assertion.
EVA: Does it mean I have to stand up to Janos? Agnes, I am afraid of him.
AGNES: (*realises*) I see. (*Pause*).
EVA: (*hesitates*) You see, once Janos abused me and hit me, I expect him to do it anytime. It is as if I wait for him to erupt in violence. It's awful. I am always on guard with him and try not to say anything which might annoy him. (*Pause*) The worst is when I lie next to him in bed, the terror of being strangled by him is so much upon me. (*Surprised by her admission*) Is this what you meant as joining forces? I never thought I would say this out to anyone.
AGNES: (*holds her hand*) You have done it now, Eva. What it means is that you have to do more.
EVA: Like what?
AGNES: To say no to Janos – a clear, confident no, that you believe in yourself; a no to being forced into having a child, a no to being beaten, a no to being sent to your mother's – a no that Janos hears and understands as no.

EVA: I don't believe I'll ever be able to say no to him. (*Agitated*) You don't understand, Agnes, I'm frightened of him but I also love him.
AGNES: How can you love him and fear him at the same time?
EVA: Because I was brought up to accept the two as one, a woman is.
AGNES: How terrible that we should have to live like that.
EVA: But we do. All the girls I know are afraid of their boyfriends, (*adding*) though they'd never admit it.

They fall silent. EVA looks at her watch.

AGNES: (*quickly*) Can you listen to one more monologue before you go? Please, Eva, it's very important to hear how women *can* say no.
EVA: (*indifferently*) The last one then. (*Picks up the script-sheets*) What is it?
AGNES: It's my Isabella's from *Measure for Measure*.

AGNES gets ready. As the monologue progresses, EVA gives up looking into the sheet and watches AGNES.

ISABELLA'S REFUSAL

Give me leave to speak, my gracious Duke,
Before this public court is dispersed and
Private festivities given full rein. Your
Stage-craft would leave the best of actors
And dramatists of our times agog with
Wonder at your incomparable skill. The
State of Vienna receives justice from
Your hands; the fates would not have fared
Better. And now amidst applause and cheers
The curtain falls on the city's high drama.

Since it's a comedy, no heads have fallen,
Instead Hymen is paraded – as punishment
Or reward is difficult to tell. And to me,
O Prince, you toss from your throne
Spousal de futuro and move on to matters
More important. A hasty proposal of marriage
Deserves a quick reply. So haste not away,
My worthy Duke, stay this distinguished
Assembly to hear my answer. To your
Proposal I say – no. No to your making
What is yours mine and mine yours. What is
Isabella's can never be yours. The reasons
For rejection are real, not spiritual,
And not open to persuasion. I mean what
I say. So, with due respect, O Duke, your
Age and temperament make you more a ruling
Father than a desiring groom for me.
Your throne is a sorry witness to misrule,
Misjudgment and miscalculation
Of human lives. The jails are filled with
Rotting youths, their muddled heads made
A game of changeling. A week was enough to
Gauge the distance between the city's stadthaus
And its brothels, between state prisons
And public courts. No, I will not return
To the Convent, from the gates of which
I was pull'd back to save this city. They say
A culture is judged by how it treats its
Women. Here in Vienna, bad or good, women
Are raped, blackmailed, humiliated, and
Declared mad when they cry out for justice.
Hence, to all present here, I announce
That from today I dedicate my life to
The cause of human rights in this sad city.

EVA rushes to AGNES and showers her with kisses.

EVA: How wonderful! A wonderful monologue, words so wonderful, thoughts so wonderful, wonderful, wonderful and wonderful, What a feeling of liberation. Oh, would that I was Isabella.

> Oh, sweet wine of words, so drunk am I on thy heady truths . . . . .

AGNES: *(chuckling)* In that case it won't be safe for you to go out.
EVA: Oh yes, it's safe for me to go out, to walk out, to fly up or down or sideways – *(singing)* wherever whenever.....
AGNES: *(testing her)* to meet Janos?
EVA: *(recklessly)* Let him wait, I am not flying to him, attend to the word – not – I pray.
AGNES: *(laughing)* I see. I'm beginning to get the message.
EVA: Come, Aliena, let's sing and be merry. Let Janos come here to find me, if he wants. Here I am, here he'll find me si..ng..gi..ng.
AGNES: *(starts singing)* Come hither, come hither, come hither: - my own song redone from Shakespeare Bacchi
EVA joins her.

O sweet Janos
O darling Peter
Here at the altar of love and fun,
We wait to lie with you in the sun.
The wind will sing and the cloud will rove
Come hither, come hither, come hi….ther:

O fiery Janos
O gentle Peter
But when we shun your desire strong,
Or temper, anger, force and throng;

Listen to our no, no-nonny no, hey-no
Come hither, come hither; come hi….ther:

O darling Janos
O sweet Peter
Why not hear no as well as yes
When love is both song and sigh
Hey nonny-no! we are nők* of nay and yea
So, come hither, come hither, come hi…ther…

We are nők of nay and yea; hey nonny-no!
Come hither, come hither, come hither…..

Singing continues. Lights fade, singing fades.

*In Hungarian, nő means woman, and nők, women.

Pilgrimage to the Cedars of Lebanon, 1907
by Tivadar Kosztka Csontváry

***An Indiaman in a Gale off a Rocky Coast*, 17th C.
by Willem van de Velde the Younger**

Play 3

Caliban

Right: programmes of the productions
performed as dramatised readings
at
The First Shakespeare Symposium
Gender Aspects of Shakespeare's Work and Age
University of the West, Timisoara, Romania 11-12th
November 2011
&
The Blue Elephant Theatre, London, on 30th June 2001

Making Good Theatre
presents
a dramatised reading of
Caliban
A sequel to Shakespeare's The Tempest
by
Rani Drew

Caliban starts where *The Tempest* ends. After the colonisers have departed, the island regains its confidence. What was seen as evil by the intruders is simply the island's pristine state. Its natural resources, its flora and fauna and its myths of gods and spirits reveal the rich social and animistic beliefs of the people. The lessons of colonial oppression are many for the islanders, as they prepare to move into another period of their history.

The First Shakespeare Symposium
Gender Aspects of Shakespeare's Work and Age
**University of West Timisoara
November 11-12, 2011**

Characters: in order of appearance

Caliban	Alex Orvatan
Ariel	Tiberiu Balint
Sycorax	Octavia Drexler
Tsilah	Christina Groza
Wutki	Lorelei Popescu
Atuki	Anamaria Birgean
Mapachitl	Iasmina Dumitriu

*same actors played other minor characters.

Production Team

Assitant Director
Roxana Ghita

Producer & Director
Rani Drew

My many thanks to Reghina Dascal for inviting me to present a dramatised reading of *Caliban* to enhance the mood of the conference. And my very grateful thanks to Roxana Ghita, who took on the burden of pre-performance preparation of selecting and preparing the actors for the occasion.

Rani Drew, a playwright, poet and short story writer, is no stranger to Romania. Her work has been published in Romanian journals as well as in literary magazines on three continents. Of her thirty or so plays, *Cleopatra,* another adaptation of Shakespeare, has been staged in six countries, being performed in Timisoara in 1999.

Two other post-Shakespearean feminist plays, *The III-Act Hamlet* and *Shakespeare & Me* were performed at festivals in Romania (in 1992 and 1995) and won prizes. Rani delivered papers on her Hamlet play at conferences in Oradea and Timisoara in 1995 and 1996 and on the politics behind a modern play of hers, *B for Beef: Buy British* at Timisoara in 1997.

The late Florentin Toma, an inspirational teacher at the Timisoara Shakespeare School, produced her *III-Act Hamlet* with his students and then published it in *The World in an Anthology* (1995). Later, Rani wrote an introduction to his translation of Marlowe's *Hero and Leander* (1999). Her story about the Cultural Revolution in China, *The Day Karl Marx was made Bald* was also translated into Romanian.

Rani's play *Caliban*, a post-colonial sequel to Shakespeare's *The Tempest,* was given its first reading-performance at the Blue Elephant Theatre in London. Tonight will be its first showing in Romania.

Her debut novel, *The Dog's Tale*, was recently published by Whytetracks, Denmark.

Hijack

NEW WRITING PROGRAMME

At the Blue Elephant Theatre

Presents a reading of

Caliban

By Rani Drew

30th June 2001

at 8pm

NEW WRITING PROGRAMME

From **18 - 30 June 2001**, the Blue Elephant Theatre is offering 4 writers of new, unperformed plays, 3 days of open access to the theatre's studio and resources.

Writers will be offered technical and artistic support from a range of theatre professionals and work with the Blue Elephant's pool of actors, presenting a 'try-out' reading/performance to an invited audience.

Caliban

Caliban is a sequel to Shakespeare's *The Tempest*, beginning where Shakespeare's play ends. After Prospero's rule ends the colonial perception of the island is dispelled. The islanders' rich social and animistic beliefs are revealed as they move into a new period of their history.

The Writer

Rani Drew's plays, including *Shakespeare & Me*, *The III-Act Hamlet* and *Cleopatra*, have been produced in China, Hungary, Romania, Spain and the UK. She has taught in universities in Singapore, China and Hungary. She is a writer of short stories and poems as well as articles on Freud, women's writings and post-colonial literature.

The Cast

Caliban	Andrew Wright
Ariel	Jonathan Voe
Sycorax	Olivia MacDonald
Wutki	Maureen Younger
Atuki	Rona Topaz
Machapitl	Simon Brignall
Tsilah	Nikki Durrant

Foreword

I have constructed *Caliban* along the lines of *The Tempest*. The integrity of Shakespeare's play is preserved in the structure, number and length of the acts. Three out of seven characters in *Caliban* are characters in *The Tempest* who belong to the Island: Ariel, Caliban and Sycorax. In Shakespeare's play Ariel and Caliban are kept apart and divided. In bringing them together, I spin out another story rather than stand *The Tempest* on its head.

The play is divided into two sections. The first half dwells on the remote and recent pasts: the exploitation of Sycorax by European sailors, and her arrival on the island, followed by the period of occupation of the island by Prospero. This changes our perception of the island from Prospero's view to Sycorax's. The themes of familial treachery, political exile, parent-offspring misunderstanding and then reconciliation remain the same as in *The Tempest*. Sycorax like Prospero is the presiding spirit of the island, but not egocentric and tyrannical like him. In CALIBAN, her first job is to reconcile Ariel and Caliban, so that together they can rebuild their island, much devastated and ill-used by the invaders. The second part departs from *The Tempest* altogether and looks to the future of the island, building up its lost culture and prosperity. In positing change, I have taken liberties with the movement of time. The play begins at the beginning of colonial times (early 1600s), but ends with the building of - what sounds like - a modern state, although only five years have passed in between.

The theme of magic is explored variously. First, magic is not seen as evil, but as an art necessary for survival against evil. Unlike Prospero's magic, which is self-centred and is used to control others to the point of slavery, Sycorax's practice of magic is for the safety and well-being of the community against the savagery of the invaders. Secondly, the magic of the island is seen more comprehensively, in its myths of gods, animals and nature. On the other side of the scale is the theme of modern xenophobia relating to the issues of migration and asylum-seeking.

The Caribbean beliefs and traditions are brought into sharp focus as the backbone of the life of the island. The belief in the transmigration of the soul is made an integral part of the story. The practice of choosing a child as the new vessel for the Island Soul is much like the Tibetan concept of rebirth of the Dalai Lama. The traditions of the island are invoked and revived after the departure of the western intruders, not simply as a return to the past, but as a step forward to a new future. By making the child of Caliban and Tsilah as the next chosen vessel of the Island Soul, I am reinforcing the historical fact of 'migrants' becoming 'native' in any national history.

The last scene of Nuptials and Carnival must be played with the energy and dynamism one associates with Caribbean culture. The numerous figures that appear in the scene are in fact the seven main characters. The scene is carefully constructed so that along with unmasked Caliban, Tsilah, Ariel and Sycorax, the masked representations of guards, evil spirits and gods (adding up to quite a few) are all played by the seven.

Caliban is a sequel to Shakespeare's *The Tempest*. It starts where Shakespeare's play ends. The colonial perception of the Caribbean is dispelled and the island is seen in its cultural diversity. Once the colonizers have departed, the island regains its confidence. What was seen as evil by the invaders is simply the island's pristine state. Its natural resources, its flora and fauna and its myths of gods and spirits reveal the rich social and animistic beliefs of the people. The lessons of colonial oppression are many for the islanders, as they prepare to move into another period of their history.

SUMMARY

1.1. The royal ship is pulling out of Bermuda harbour, taking Prospero and Miranda, and all the characters that make up Shakespeare's story of *The Tempest*. Left behind on the island are the two natives, Ariel and Caliban, both enslaved and exploited by Prospero for his own purposes. They had never met each other while their master held sway over them. Now left alone with each other, they don't know how to respond or react to one another. Ariel hates Caliban and sees him as savage; and Caliban, as the owner of the island, wants Ariel to be his slave.

1.2. Sycorax appears to Caliban, her son, and relates the story of how she was lured by treasure-seeking European sailors from her father's kingdom in Algiers, and eventually abandoned on the island. The islanders accepted her as one of their own, even honouring her as a healer. After a few years, when she spotted a ship approaching the island, to save the people from the sailors' ruthless ways, she put a spell on everyone, including him and Ariel, which was to be lifted only after the departure of the intruders. Now the island can wake to its past well-being. She asks Caliban to seek out Ariel as she has to tell him important things about the island.

2.1. At first, Ariel is as hostile to Sycorax as Prospero was, but slowly he comes to see her as a benign spirit. As Sycorax reveals more truths to him, he makes up with Caliban. They promise to work together for the future of the island. Sycorax tells Ariel about the tradition of the Island Soul. She can now pass away in peace.

3.1. A comic interlude. Five years have passed. The island is a republic and economically prosperous. But too much hard work has turned the workers to rebellion against Caliban, who is now in charge of agriculture. A worker, Mapachitl, incites them against Caliban, who, he says, is an immigrant to the island and should not be given preference over the natives. He urges them to take their complaints to Ariel, who is the President of the Nation. A deputation sets off to see Ariel.

3.2. Ariel is with his sister Tsilah, who has to be told that her marriage with Caliban was pre-determined by Sycorax, and that it is for the good of the Carib Nation. Tsilah likes Caliban, but does not want to marry him because of his ugliness. What she does not know is that Caliban, like the Frog Prince, became ugly because of a spell. The condition for Caliban's restoration to good looks is marriage with Tsilah.

4.1. The workers' deputation arrives and as they are airing their grievances, Caliban enters. There is an ugly scene about Caliban's nationality. Mapachitl objects to an immigrant being favoured over a native for the hand of Tsilah. Tsilah now realises that good looks are not everything, and chooses Caliban over Mapachitl.

4.2. Ariel leaves Tsilah to break the news to Caliban. As she tells him of her love, Caliban is restored to his pristine handsome looks.

5.1. The National Day is being celebrated with a Bermuda-style Carnival: masks, music and dances. Evil spirits are chased away and the gods and goddesses are invited to bless the nuptials. In the crowd Ariel spots Sycorax, who has come from the world of the dead to see the nuptials of her son. Ariel tells her he too would be with her soon.

CHARACTERS: in order of appearance.

CALIBAN, in his mid-twenties, is the same age as in *The Tempest*. When the play begins he is like his old self under Prospero, but he starts to change as he learns the truths about himself and the island from Sycorax, his mother. From Act 3.1, he is transformed into a totally different self: responsible, confident in work but shy with women on account of his ugly looks, which are not restored to him until the penultimate scene.

SYCORAX, in her mid-forties, is the mother of Caliban, the witch Prospero maligns so distastefully. On the contrary, we come to see her differently. She is knowledgeable, compassionate and, unlike Prospero, humble and self-critical.

ARIEL, in his late twenties, is the same as in *The Tempest*. After his initial hatred and contempt for Caliban, he changes towards him under the influence of Sycorax. He comes to realise that Prospero was a self-centred human being and a cruel master. Ariel occupies a central position in the island, and lives up to it in every way.

WUTKI & ATUKI, in their thirties, are two peasant labourers. They are a bit simple in their speech and understanding of things. They provide the comic relief and also the turning point in the story.

MAPACHITL in his late twenties, is tall and good-looking, confident but vengeful. He is a trouble-maker and xenophobic. He suffers from a mean mentality.

TSILAH, in her early twenties, is intelligent, good-looking, sweet-tempered, strong-willed and perceptive in recognising goodness when it comes her way.

Act I

Scene i

Sound of gunfire and some music to announce the sailing of the royal ship. Noises can be heard of commands being given. The curtain goes up on a stage suggestive of higher ground, a hill from where you look down on the sea. The scene is that of a jungle and overgrowth, a tall cedar tree on the left on a spur, a distinct mark of the island.

CALIBAN rushes in, having climbed up the hill to look at the coast below. He is in great excitement as he is shouting and yelling at the ship moving out to sea. He runs from side to side, from tree to tree, shouting curses and obscenities at the ship below.

CALIBAN: Yare, yare, thieves, robbers, go home, away, leave me in peace. Ahoy, boatswain, take them fast, away from this island. Away, away, faster, faster, faster *(rows to show them how fast)*. A pox on the pirates; blow winds, blow winds, blister them full; rise, sea, rise and swallow them wholesale - ha, ha, whole sail, all sails. Setebos, send wild winds, swell up the sails, rent them into shreds with tempests and retribution. Ahoy, wild winds, swirl their ship, toss Prospero from stem to stem, sling him off the ship, get him, Setebos, get him, avenge me on the whole lot. This is my only chance. Drunks and rioters, no safe journey for you. Red plague, get them in mid-ocean: the king *(spits)* & ho, ho, the wise Gonzalo *(spits)* and the magician Prospero *(spits many times, stamps and grinds)*. Setebos, bring on your storms now, show me them tossing on the swelling waves, no, no better show me their shipwreck, push them all down, thirteen fathoms deep *(enjoying the wording of every calamity)* Rise, O mighty whirlpool, and suck them, swoooooooosh, down they go to the bottom of the sea, to the pit of the ocean *(dances, stops and looks out again).*

ARIEL rushes in, waving some books at the moving ship.

ARIEL: *(shouting)* Stop, Master. Master, stop, your books are with me, you have forgotten them.
CALIBAN: *mocking)* Fly, Spirit, fly, be gone to thy master. Dost thou not see his ship yonder, taking him back to Milan, his home? Not yours, ha, ha, he hast left thou behind. Ooo, shall thou now obey him, fly through the air, swift on the ocean wide?
ARIEL: Get thee hence, vile monster, away from me. Thou art truly repulsive.
CALIBAN: *(mimicking)* Like I was to thy master? O, sweet servility, like death thou never dies. I saw liberty fallen by the wayside, and freedom weeping tears by the gallon. Tut, tut, poor Ariel! *(Snatches the books from ARIEL)*
ARIEL: Give them back, thou knowest nothing of letters. Uncouth art thou, savage by nature.
CALIBAN: Ah, nature, Mother Nature, my mother, or your mother, this island's mother? Where art thou, mother? Didst thou have a mother? Or a father? Ah, me remembers now, wast thou not born in a tree, this tree, wast that not so? Speak, Spirit. Thou wast so taught by thy master: he found you up this tree, locked up in the cloven pine, imprisoned. Werest thou? A lie, many lies that charlatan told you, didn't he? And that it was my mother, my poor mother who had imprisoned you there. And he, the great man, freed you from her spells. And thou believest

his lies.
ARIEL: Or truth? Who can sift lies from truth? Dost thou?
It matters not now. The winds take my master.
These books I wouldst carry to him, flying to
his sailing vessel, but alas, my lightness
is grounded. Gravitation proves my better friend.
Besides, I cannot order myself, my orders
must come from others; I have my freedom,
but what can I do with it? Where should I fly?
Who can order me now?
CALIBAN: *(like a lord)*   I can order you.
I am the king now, and you are my servant.
What wouldst thou want to do, eh, slave?
ARIEL: No slave to you, savage Caliban.
With no knowledge of spells and magic,
what can you command?
CALIBAN: *(bitter)*   A lot, but that was
before Prospero, like a leech, sucked all
the goodness out of me, and made me
part with all the secrets of this island,
and all the knowledge of the flora and fauna.
Like a malignant ogre, he sucked my blood,
and then put me on the scrap heap, leaving
me grovelling and begging for crumbs
to keep myself alive. That was the man
you, his sycophant, think was my better.
And although now I am the sole owner
of this island, I can give no more commands
than a blithering idiot could. But be
that as it may, *(ordering)* I command thee to wash
my feet, and fetch my food, bring me air too,
yes, quick, and bring me light, make this forest
sunny and bright. Go on, with speed, put this
island right for Caliban. See, I can order.
ARIEL: Oh, what a sorry sight of base vileness
you make. Delusions are your very nature,
savage beast. I leave you to wallow in them.

CALIBAN: What wilt thou do? Pine away, longing
 for the tyrant who has abandoned you?
ARIEL: He didst not. It was my longing for freedom
 that made him set me free. If I wished to go
 with him, he wouldst have taken me.
CALIBAN: (*mocking him*) Why didst
 he not then? O poor Ariel, thou knowest
 thou wast abandoned. Cast to the winds,
 like those books thou holdst so close to thy
 heart. Dost thou know why?
ARIEL: I asked him for
 freedom. I made him keep his promise.
CALIBAN: No, because he cheated thee, knowst thou?
 He didst not know any magic, only thou
 knewest. But he made you think it was he
 the master and you his slave.
ARIEL: (*challenging*)) Wast thou
 not the same? Me to do his magic spells
 and you his chores? We both were slaves:
 but he loved me and hated you.
CALIBAN: (*passionately*) Because you
 were the willing one, like a parrot obeying
 whatever he commanded you. I hated him.
ARIEL: And I hated you.
CALIBAN: Why dost thou hate me?
ARIEL: Because you are savage, unlearned and dull
 of senses. Prospero was right.
CALIBAN: Perfect slave
 of a perfect tyrant. From him thou learnt
 to hate me. And yet we were the only
 two natives of this land. In all the twelve years
 Prospero was here thou never spoke with me.
 What sayest to this?
ARIEL: I have nothing to say
 to you. We are from different mothers,
 that's certain.
CALIBAN: Prospero told me who wast
 my mother. He said she was a witch. Didst

he tell you about yours? Had you a mother
or a father, or were you born of none,
since thou art a spirit, eh, Ariel?
Yet, this island is ours, yours and mine,
and Prospero has sailed away. He kept
us apart when he was here, and he hath
left us apart, divided and in conflict
over nothing. And there are no others,
brother, just you and me.
ARIEL: *(desperate)* There must be some,
must be others on the island. I'll go
in search of them. It is hateful to be
with you. Don't touch those books, let go,
rude beast; such filthy hands and mind you have.

ARIEL takes a swift jump and snatches the books from CALIBAN, and exits. CALIBAN bursts out laughing and then crying.

Scene ii

Suddenly CALIBAN's name is called out. A whisper 'Caliban', 'Caliban' fills the air. CALIBAN listens. He tries to work out where the voice is coming from, and walks around. A big noise is heard from the tree, and then a thud, as if something heavy has fallen down. A youngish woman looking like a big fungus emerges. CALIBAN is shocked, overwhelmed. SYCORAX peels off the fungus layers, and motions to him to come closer to her. CALIBAN is hesitant.

SYCORAX: Fear me not, Caliban. I am Sycorax, thy mother.
CALIBAN: Sycorax, my mother! Whereof thou thus emerge, mother?
SYCORAX: Before thine eyes, from this tree, my home, for more than a decade. The wizard has gone, hasn't he? I heard you throwing curses and spells at his ship. Did

they work?
CALIBAN: *(hopeless)* No, they didn't. Didst thou teach me
your art? Hadst thou done it, Prospero would
have been fitly revenged and drowned in the sea.
What now, mother? Why here, and wherefore
call me son after long years of slavery
and suffering I endured?
SYCORAX: Believe me, my son,
I couldn't have come to your aid before.
Bound by my own spell, I had to remain
stuck in the tree, until Prospero left,
and you came within my hearing. We are
prey to the Fates, and cannot wake or die
before our times. Dost thou understand?
CALIBAN: By and by, I will, Mother. Tell me more.
I am joyous that my mother is more than
a memory. Come, touch your Caliban,
and confirm that my mind is not beset
by hallucinations.
SYCORAX: *(comes closer)* I am too real to be
just air. I too longed for my flesh and blood.
CALIBAN: Prospero made you out as a witch, and not
worthy of love. And yet thou art beautiful
and so gentle. Why am I so ugly?
SYCORAX: You are not what you look, but you must wait
before you find out, Caribima.
CALIBAN: Not Caliban?
SYCORAX: That was Prospero's name for you. The islands
in this ocean the sailors said were full
of cannibals. He thought changing the name
of the only islander he found living would rid
him of the fear of being eaten. So he called
you Caliban.
CALIBAN: I will ask Setebos
to make a meal of him, eat him limb by
limb; that will teach him a lesson. Why
didst thou not use your magic to destroy
the loathsome tyrant? Why, all those years

you watched him turn your son into a beast,
and did nothing? How could you, mother?
SYCORAX:
Let anger not spoil our long-awaited
meeting.
CALIBAN: Such foul temper that man had. All
the gruesome lies he made up about your
youth and my birth. The red plague will get him.
Often I heard him threaten poor Ariel
with your name and witchcraft, which he
said you had brought from Algiers. Is that
true?
SYCORAX: True it was. In Algiers I was known
for my special gift. That was before I
was allured away by an adventurer,
and later left here. Presently, I shall
tell thee my story. Oh, such pain I feel
to see you stand there, looking so savage.
Slavery and oppression did the worst
for you. But I'm to blame for it.
CALIBAN: How now,
mother? Why blame thyself for others' misdoings?
It was Prospero's cruel and unkind nature.
Joy is now mine to see my mother stand
before me. Tell me how you came from Algiers
to this Island.
SYCORAX: Listen then. There was a time
when I was the only daughter of the king
of Algiers. I wore royal tiaras as haloes round
my head. My father had a kingdom of gold.
The tales of its wealth and abounding riches
were carried to other lands; thereby, a constant
flow of seafarers washed up on our coast,
pretending to be ship-wrecked; but in truth,
looking for the renowned treasures. Trails
of greed furrowed the seas. But the king
was wise and ever remained wary of all
strangers. At the slightest suspicion,

he would put them under arrest, and if
further proof came to light, executed them
at once.

CALIBAN: I wish he had done it to Prospero;
I would have been spared the degradation
he made mine. But carry on.

SYCORAX: Then one day
a ship anchored in our harbour. The sailors
were taken into custody immediately
and questioned as to their purpose of landing
on our coast. Their tongues, sweetened with
flattery, spun out stories of exiles
and tragedies, but the king was ruled by
caution against greed and pillage by European
fleets. He eschewed their explanations,
and ordered execution of the leader, and
the rest, he announced, would serve his state
as slaves.

CALIBAN: How many?

SYCORAX: Over a hundred,
not counting the galley slaves. I was
present when he decreed the chief of the ship
be put to death. As I looked at the marked man,
I was overcome by compassion. He
commanded a good physique and a handsome
visage. In that instant, what took hold of me
I do not know to this day. I who was
renowned for my knowledge of nature's
secrets, felt myself in the power of this
stranger. He had fixed his eyes on me;
and as if under a spell, I heard myself
mutter full that I must save the fated man.

CALIBAN: Oh, mother.

SYCORAX: Yes, so blind I was with something,
I did not know what. Like one gone mad,
I got busy with a plan of rescue.
To see him free and escape unharmed
became the only thing I could think of.

He must escape, leave our coast with his men,
without being harmed, I repeated to myself.
Secretly, I sent him a message
to tell him I had plans. He promised
to take me with him, swearing he
could not live without me. Oh, fates that blind
you, and Cupid whose arrows bleed your sanity,
clear the way for tragedy.

CALIBAN: Was it
    a tragedy in the end?

SYCORAX: Not while the high
    tide of passion lasted. My dull life
    had made me long for adventure
    away on the high sea; shore-bound I
    had been for years. O stubborn desire that
    leads us astray.

CALIBAN: Whereto wert thou led?

SYCORAX: To betrayal and deception that held me
    ransom to the king's decree. That night
    I stole up to his cell, giving some lie
    to the guards. He knew I would come
    and was ready to bolt. He asked if I had
    brought my jewels with me. I should have
    known then, that it were my jewels and not
    me he coveted. He had maddened me so,
    I could have slain the guards if they had
    attempted to bar my flight.

CALIBAN: Heavens, mother!

SYCORAX: The Heavens were conspiring against me, as I
    held the torch to lead him out of the prison
    to the harbour, through the alleys where no
    one waked. The boat was there, the guards
    keeping watch over the sailors. I cast
    a spell over them, versed in magic, it was child's
    play to put them to sleep until the boat moved
    away to the sea. We boarded without a hitch!
    The sailors were ready with their oars, and my
    servants carried food and drink on to the boat.

> I repaid them with coins and a promise
> not to own up to anything, for their own good.
> I wanted no mark left in the trail. They were
> hardly gone, when the boat pulled away,
> the sails were unfurled and I rode the high
> waves of freedom and passion.

CALIBAN: You were not afraid of retribution?

SYCORAX: I was with the gods,
> in supreme joy. The laughter too was ours.
> The sailor loved me, and I him. The world
> was one and the same for us – willowy and
> ever in motion. Together, we watched
> the sun and the moon over the ocean.
> Oh, fickle happiness, were you ever there?

CALIBAN: Am I the sailor's son, Mother?

SYCORAX: I wish
> you were. He might not have abandoned me
> then.

CALIBAN: But I am your child?

SYCORAX: One I am proud of.
> Listen, there is more to tell. The sails
> had caught the wind and moved fast, well
> out of the reach of the king's forces. The world
> lay at my feet. Before a full moon came
> round again, I found myself with child.
> The fates struck me most cruelly. The sailor
> suspected it was not his child and turned
> away from me, abandoned me to pine
> for him. Isolated by tongue and culture
> from all on board, I wished I had never
> left home. But the winds went before us,
> there was no turning back. I tried my spells
> to stoke the dying passion in him; he grew
> suspicious, and stopped coming to me. I was
> left to myself. We sailed for what seemed
> a long time, then one day we anchored at an
> island. The natives, a strange-looking people,

stood hostile on the shore. He pointed to me
and through gestures indicated that he
was going to leave me with them. And then
a boat was launched to take me ashore. I
lived up to my royal pride and remained
dry-eyed.
CALIBAN: Had I known, I would have strangled
Prospero.
SYCORAX: On the shore I stood and saw the boat
sail away. And my jewels with it.
CALIBAN: Thieves!
SYCORAX: What use would they have been on the
island? The natives knew of no such ware.
They took me to be a gift from the ocean,
a gift from Yamalla, their goddess of the sea.
Immediately, I was taken to their shaman,
an old woman, much respected by them.
CALIBAN: Setebos was with you.
SYCORAX: The old woman
at once sensed my knowledge of magic,
and took me under her wings. Fates were
smiling on me again. For a while I
pined for the sailor and his sweet embraces,
and the child growing within me.
CALIBAN: But thou
denyest I was the sailor's seed.
SYCORAX: It was not you.
One day the sailor's seed dropped out of me,
just like that. I did not feel any sorrow.
The chief of the tribe wanted me, the old
woman gave the go-ahead. We lay together,
and you took root.
CALIBAN: You became one of them.
SYCORAX: And you were one of them.
CALIBAN: A true Carib,
Caribima. What went wrong, mother,
that the island became so desolate?
SYCORAX: This is what I must tell you now. Where is

Ariel? To him, I must impart something
vital, before departing from this world.
CALIBAN: Ariel hates me so, but I will go
and look for him.
SYCORAX: No stay, Caribima,
there is more to tell. Time is short. Soon
a new life overtook my past. Shaman
Atekosang passed on her magic lore to me.
When she performed rituals and used spells
to tap nature's power for the general good,
I was always with her. I soon became
well-versed in the beliefs of the islanders.
Five years thus passed. You were growing up fast.
One day, the old woman told me that she
was going to die shortly, and must tell me
about the belief in the transmigration
of the soul.
CALIBAN: What does that mean? Prospero said
nothing about a soul.
SYCORAX: Of such things he
knew nothing. The body dies but the soul
is immortal. At the time of death
the dead man's soul transmigrates into
a new being.
CALIBAN: A strange belief.
SYCORAX: Not strange
when you understand it. She pronounced
that her soul would be reborn in the child
whose birth was imminent, born to a woman,
far gone in pregnancy. She said this was
how it had been happening on the island
from times immemorial.
CALIBAN: And you saw
it happening?
SYCORAX: I did. She instructed me
how her funeral rites should be arranged,
and how they should coincide with the birth
of the new-born who was to receive her

soul. Then she called a meeting of the elders
and announced that the office of the shaman
would be invested in me, until the child
came of age. They bowed to her wish. The
mother was sought out and informed of what
was to come. There was excitement among
the people. A dance was held to give thanks
to Eleggua, the deity of links between the old
and the new, who maintains the cycle of death
and birth. And I was representing him.
CALIBAN: Such honour and trust. I am proud of you.
SYCORAX: As the child started to move through the birth
canal the old woman began to breath her last.
When the first cry of the infant was heard, her
heart became still. The funeral ceremony was
combined with the birth celebration. After a huge
platform was built and the bier was placed
on it, the newly-born was made to light
the fire. The ancient musical instruments were
sounded and sacred hymns chanted for her
journey to the other world. While the flames
were rapidly consuming the bier, songs were
sung and drums were beaten to welcome
the old soul into the new.
CALIBAN: I can feel it.
SYCORAX: Sport and games followed; competitions
were held and winners awarded; the couples
were matched and prizes awarded to the best.
CALIBAN: Did I win any games? I would have liked
to have a partner.
SYCORAX: At the age of five?
CALIBAN: Damn. And who was the child?
SYCORAX: Ariel.
CALIBAN: Oh, Ariel again. At least it makes him younger
than me.
SYCORAX: But also older, much older,
as old as the island itself. You have
only your own age, he carries the lives

of many souls before him.
CALIBAN: Does a soul have age?
SYCORAX: In migrating from one body to another, it accumulates both the individual's goodness and its experiences; thus adding years to its own age. Dost thou understand now?
CALIBAN: I am trying to. Why is no one alive now?
SYCORAX: I am coming to that. Some years passed. The chief, your father, died of fever. Another chief was chosen, but I did not take up with him. I was officiating as the shaman, and also keeping an eye on the Island Soul.
CALIBAN: That's Ariel. And me?
SYCORAX: Growing fast, in leaps and bounds. Fair and bright, you were my own Caribima.
CALIBAN: Don't mock me, mother.
SYCORAX: The truth will soon be out. All those years, Setebos, the god of the Caribs protected you from harms. But when the Fates run amuck, even the gods give in. Five happy years passed – I counted from the almanack I had made from memory, my mind still worked off numbers, old habits die hard – that's when misfortune struck the island.
CALIBAN: I was ten. See, I too can count. That tyrant did me some good.
SYCORAX: Not to us. From this hill I spotted the ship coming towards our island. With Yamalla's help, I invoked raging winds and fierce tempests to stop their advance. But it was too late. The ship was fast heading this way. Old memories were stirred and I panicked. I rang the drum and fetched the elders

up here. For the first time I told my story
to them, and warned them of the terrible
greed and deceit of the seafaring people.
They looked to me for advice. I said the best
way would be for me to cast a spell on all
of us, so that when the sailors found
the island desolate they would move on.
The elders welcomed the idea. I laid
my plan before them: I would make
everyone invisible, blend them
with the natural growth of the island; Ariel
I would hide in the cleft of this tall tree,
and myself just under it, as a poisonous
fungus, so that no one could come near Ariel.
They all agreed.
CALIBAN: What did you do with me?
SYCORAX: You are too impatient. While the sailors
were dropping anchor in the bay, I was
casting Loas' spell on the islanders.
Next I put Ariel in the care of Aguara,
and then only I put Agaman Nibo's spell
on myself, and became a fungus.
CALIBAN: And me?
What did you do with me? What spell did you
put on me?
SYCORAX: You I was going to put
in care of Ayizan, the guardian
goddess of doorways and gates, but the evil
spirits intercepted the spell. To overcome
their magic, I changed to another spell,
to turn you into a prickly bush
so that the invaders could not harm you.
CALIBAN: I would have pricked Prospero to death.
SYCORAX: This angered the Diablesse. They speeded up
the spell on me, and I turned into the fungi
on the cedar even before I could complete
my magic on you; the next moment, I saw
you turn into a savage, the only human

on the island.
CALIBAN: O wretched, pitiless fate.
SYCORAX: A mother's fate. For twelve years I saw
you becoming worse through oppression.
O son, it was terrible to watch the tyrant
treat you worse than a slave.
CALIBAN: Forget the past.
Change me to my original form, mother,
quick, do it now, I can't wait any longer.
SYCORAX: Curse your mother, Caribima, whose fate
you inherited. The angry gods decreed:
I may never again see my fair child.
CALIBAN: Why dost thou need to obey them, Mother?
SYCORAX: Because I failed in my spell.
CALIBAN: I must pay
for it?
SYCORAX: Sadly, you must. You must perform
some labours first, for which a reward
will be given to you, along with a
return to your original form.
CALIBAN: Your gods
are as cruel as that tyrant. Constant
slavery is my fate.
SYCORAX: What you will do for this island will not
be slavery but service to your people.
CALIBAN: Where are these people?
SYCORAX: I shall soon lift
the spell, and this island will awake
to the sound of people, birds and beasts.
But first, I must see Ariel. Where is he?
CALIBAN: Thanks to you, he runs away from my ugly sight.
SYCORAX: It could be worse. Fetch Ariel, time
is running out. You must find him. Go.

CALIBAN exits, calling out Ariel's name repeatedly, 'Ariel', 'Where are you?'

SYCORAX: A mother's woe to see her son so depraved.

Caliban

Worse, I shan't be here to see him beaming
at his own bright visage.
      O Setebos,
 God of the Patagonians, help me
 to invoke all the gods of the Caribs
 to hasten the process of revival
 on this island.

     O Obbuddumare,
 Spirit of Creation, come to my aid
 and stir the dreaming life on this island.
 Let nothing go wrong in the lifting
 of the spell. I submit to your supreme
 power for guidance to my swan song.

In each of the four corners, she invokes gods, guardians of various aspects of nature and living beings. After every invocation, the stir of life is heard in the call of birds and beasts, daily noises of human chores, the sound of the drum and tribal singing of the people.

  Shango, God of the Ocean, you who rule
  the waters all the way to Africa,
  from coast to coast, guard the island against
  pirates and seafarers. Let tempests, winds
  and lightning send terror and destruction
  on mercenaries and adventurers
  that dare ride your mighty waves.

  Oya, Goddess of fire and thunderbolt,
  help Shango when invaders are sighted.
  With gusts of winds smash their vessels, set fire
  to their sails and scorch them with your bolts.
  Stop them from coming to our shores. Let
  no one land here who covets our island.

  Yamalla, you link the moon with the ocean
  and make the waters swell to mighty waves,

even so, help me now to awaken
all the beings I once put to sleep.
Rise and awake, O tribe of the Caribs,
the invaders have gone. Our Yamalla
will fill you with plenty, and increase
your tribe, like the waxing of her moon.

And now, Oshun, you I invoke. Bring out
your arrows of love and desire; make them
mad with your touch. Let no one resist you,
Oshun, O goddess of sweet agony,
your pleasures are in excess and many.

Having propitiated all the gods and goddesses of the four regions, Sycorax now stands in the centre and invokes Obatala, the god of peace and beauty. The island is fully awakened.

O Obatala, god of peace and beauty,
make the Caribs as your favoured children.
Fill their hearts with love and desire, light their
homes and hearths with wealth and prosperity.

Lastly, Eleggua, messenger spirit
between the living and the immortals,
favour the Caribs in your tales to the
gods. O master magician, invoke the
best spells when new plans are made,
clear all obstacles from the way, and
make success smile its best on the island.

Running feet are heard.

Hark! That must be Ariel. I must hide.

Act II

Scene i

ARIEL rushes in, fleeing the calls of CALIBAN, 'Ariel', 'Ariel', which now recede. Exhausted, he collapses under the tree and holds his head in despair

ARIEL: O, cruel fates that leave me at Caliban's mercy! O Heavenly Spirits, protect me from his savage voice.

SYCORAX comes out from behind the tree and calls Ariel by his name. ARIEL looks up and is startled by her looks. He jumps up and wants to run away.

SYCORAX: Ariel, hear me. I am Sycorax. Canst thou see me?
ARIEL: O heavens, witch Sycorax, art thou she who kept me prisoner in this pine for a decade-long span? What wilt thou now want of me, witch?
SYCORAX: Thou were told lies, Ariel. It's time to remove the tarnish that hath made the truth so black. Prospero was a liar.
ARIEL: No, thou art false, thy witchcraft black, Satan's own art. Begone, witch, thou reeks of evil.
SYCORAX: Ariel, shortly I must die. If thou does not pay heed to me, thou wilt regret, for no one else knows what I do. Will thou listen now?
ARIEL: With caution.
SYCORAX: Then heed my words. Thou art of this island, older than me,

older than this tree, older even than
this forest. You are as old as the bare
bones of this island, born with it as it
rose out of the ocean.
ARIEL: Come, come, let's not
dabble in words, and wear masks to hide
our true selves. I know I am no older
than two decades. Prospero told me.
SYCORAX: What did
Prospero know of this island? Would
that he had not heard you crying. Suffering
might have been better than all that
obedience and slavery you had at his
hands, which killed your native spirit.
ARIEL: Far from it,
it made me know someone better than you.
He was wrathful and tyrannical, even cruel
at times but more human. He was a better
magician than you.
SYCORAX: He deceived you, made
you repeat all the magic lore you knew,
and pretended to be a magician
himself. A few spells he brought with him
he had learnt from books, read in candlelight
in dark palaces. Unlike this island,
nature's abode, which is steeped in the magic
of the unseen, the unbelieved. Here there are
no books, no learning of words, but nature,
vibrant and live beyond our understanding.
Did Prospero know of the funeral rites,
of fire, water, the cycles of life and death,
when souls leave one vessel and enter another?
ARIEL: I understand not what thou sayest. Explain.
SYCORAX: (*Whispers*) Ariel, dost thou remember a funeral?
(*waits*) Dost thou? Close your eyes and see if big
flames light the darkness of your mind?
ARIEL: *(closes eyes)* Some shadows flicker. Fierce flames

leap in the dark, figures are moving, sounds
of lament and chants rising to the skies. *(Waits)*
Nothing more. It stops there.
SYCORAX: The rest is lost
to you in the years you spent with Prospero.
Your memory is tinged with fake spells. The fires
you see flickering are of a very important
funeral rite when you were just born. It
took place before Prospero's ship anchored
in our harbour.
ARIEL: Didst thou not land the same way?
SYCORAX:
I did, but not willingly. I was put down
here, abandoned, like an unwanted pet.
ARIEL: And pregnant with that loathsome child.
SYCORAX: That child died inside me.
ARIEL: Did the islanders
not shun you?
SYCORAX: Far from that. They soon sensed that I had
knowledge of magic, I was taken to their
shaman, the old woman. She took me
under her wing. As sisters in metaphysics
we soon discovered that our roots went back
to mythical times. I became even more
special as the chief of the tribe wanted
me for himself. Within a year, I gave
birth to Caribima, whom you learnt
to call Caliban. You played together,
as childhood mates.
ARIEL: I couldn't have, not with
that creature.
SYCORAX: You were taught to hate him
by Prospero. He kept you apart. Caribima
is fair of looks and of gentle nature
as much as thou art, and of this island.
The truth will be out one day. Now, to more
urgent matters. For a decade all life
on this island – people, birds and beasts –

were put under a spell to save them from
the foul play of the alien sailors.
ARIEL: It is you then who made this island barren.
SYCORAX: Not barren but invisible until
the strangers departed. Though not seen,
all beings remained alive. It was for their
sounds and stirrings that the invaders
feared the island and called it the Devil's own.
I had learnt not to trust them from bitter
experience and would not have the same
happen to this beautiful haven.
ARIEL: If that
was so, why was I left at their mercy?
SYCORAX: You weren't. I wanted to protect you more,
and keep you separate from others, and under
my close watch. But Fate went against me, and
the spell used to conceal you went wrong.
Wouldst that you had not cried out, the stranger
would not have heard you. When he tried
to climb the tree, I showered him
with poisonous fumes. He then got
'Caliban' to go up and get you; a native's
life wasn't worth a groat. But how could I
poison my own son? So, I saw him take you
down and could do nothing. It is my son you
have to thank, and not Prospero, for what
you call freedom.
ARIEL: And a spell on Caliban too?
SYCORAX: On him also. Setebos let me down.
You were heard whimpering in the
tall cedar and my son found stamping
the earth like a savage.
ARIEL: Was it not a pine
where I was hid?
SYCORAX: No, a cedar it was.
Prospero knew little of this island's
flora.
ARIEL: *(aside: O Master)* And the island still lies

in oblivion?
SYCORAX: Not so now. Slowly
you will understand when you live among
the people. Listen! You can hear them now.

Sounds of people are heard.

ARIEL: And is the shaman among them?
SYCORAX: Sadly not.
Shaman Atekoshang died when you
were born. Her death and your birth were one
and the same thing. The fires flickering
in your memory are the funeral
rites of shaman Atekoshang; she was
known as the Island Soul.
ARIEL: Why was she called
the Island Soul?
SYCORAX: Because her age was not
her own, but the age of the island from
the beginning of Time. In her were all
the shamans who had lived here before her.
As one shaman died, her soul entered a new-
born, chosen by her as the next Island Soul.
In this way, a continuity is maintained;
each time the body is new but the soul is old.
When I came to know her she was already
getting old, and wanted to teach me what
she knew, but also learn things from me.
One day, after five years - Caribima
was five by then - and Prospero had
not yet arrived, she declared she
was going to die on a certain day, which
was the day you were to be born. She
had chosen you as the new vessel
for the Island Soul.
ARIEL: Me? Why?
SYCORAX: You were barely
conceived, but Atekoshang knew it. She

set a day nine months later, when her death
and your birth would coincide, to facilitate
the transmigration of the soul from one being
into another.
ARIEL: These are strange ways unheard of.
SYCORAX: Only because you have been corrupted
into thinking with your head rather than
your heart.
ARIEL: And for this was the funeral rite?
SYCORAX: A double celebration of the cycle
of death and life. The fire is the symbol
of purification of the dying
into the living. Those images that
you see flaring are the earliest
impressions your infant mind absorbed.
They are not to be feared.
ARIEL: Then what happened?
SYCORAX: Five more years passed. People died, children
were born, we sang and danced, tilled and harvested
as do any people of the land. Then one day, I saw
a ship advancing towards the island.
My memories of another ship had
not dimmed. I feared for the islanders
and our life here. In agreement with
with the elders, I put a safety lock
on the island, casting a spell on
everyone, to be lifted at the departure
of the strangers. You know the rest.
ARIEL: The Island
Soul, eh? What do you want me to do now?
SYCORAX: First, you must make friends with Caribima.
He will be the body of this island, and you
its spirit. The island has woken from
a long slumber. People will want someone
to guide them to a new life. The island
must return to its old prosperity.
Caribima must show them how to farm
the barren landscape. The trees must bear fruit,

        the earth grain and rivers must water them.
        Birds will sing and bees will pollinate
        plants and flowers, and beasts will enrich
        the forests to greater numbers. The people
        will look to Caribima and you, and soon
        well-being and prosperity will dwell
        among us as the wind does in the ocean.
ARIEL: And you, what will happen to you?
SYCORAX: My time
        is up. The invaders have left, the island
        is awake. I shall now depart from this life
        to return to Setebos's land. He is waiting
        for me. You and Caribima must make sure
        that my funeral fires leap high and fierce,
        and end in traditional festivities.
        The future of the island is in your
        joined hands.
ARIEL: And your soul? What will happen to it?
SYCORAX: I shall be reborn, in what form I come
        back to the living will depend on my
        deeds in this life.
ARIEL: And Caribima, when will
        the spell lift off him? You spoke of some reward?
        What is that? You must tell before departing.
SYCORAX: In five years' time, this island will be
        a paradise. This is the task for Caribima,
        his responsibility to restore it to its past.
        After that he will receive his reward.
ARIEL: *(panicking)* How? What? speak?
SYCORAX: He was promised to Tsilah by the Old Woman.
ARIEL: Who is Tsilah? And where is she?
SYCORAX: Tsilah
        was born the year before the sailors arrived.
        She was thy sister.
ARIEL: My sister to marry
        Caliban?
SYCORAX: The Old Woman predicted her birth

ARIEL: She too was put under a spell?
SYCORAX: She was. Named after the goddess of beauty and fortune, she was changed into a wild flower, with medicinal value. Now back to her original self, like everyone else, she will bring forth new beings to increase the wealth of the island of Carios.
ARIEL: With Caliban?
SYCORAX: Yes, with Caribima, my son. Promise me, Ariel.
ARIEL: I promise, if I understand any of your riddles. *(Hesitant)* And me, am I to enter wedlock too?
SYCORAX: Wedlock is not for you. For this reason, you were chosen as the Island Soul. The Old Woman knew you would be neither Man nor Woman, hence, no nuptials need be performed for you. Do you understand?

SILENCE

ARIEL: Aye, I do. *(To himself)* Miranda stirred no feelings in me. I hardly spoke to her. How strange that the Shaman knew. *(To her)* Was she one herself, I mean, like me?
SYCORAX: Your thought is far-reaching. She seemed a woman to me, but now I can see what you say.

CALIBAN is heard coming in the distance, still calling out 'Ariel', 'Ariel'. He is exhausted.

Here comes Caliban.
CALIBAN: Mother, I can't find Ariel anywhere. *(Sees him)* By Setebos, why can't you answer, Ariel?
SYCORAX: Caribima, Ariel knows everything.

> From now on, you will have to be like brothers,
> two parts of the same body. The island
> needs you both. Come, join hands in one
> vow that you will work to the good of this
> island. Caribima, you must listen to Ariel
> as a voice of wisdom, and Ariel you must
> look to Caribima as the heart of the Caribs.
> You must plan together and make this island
> an oceanic paradise. My time is up.

They do as she asks them. As they turn to each other, SYCORAX goes behind the tree.

ARIEL: Caliban – Caribima, forgive my outrages.
CALIBAN: And you my arrogance. From now on we share all things on this island.
ARIEL: Except one.
CALIBAN: What's that?
ARIEL: You'll find out in time. Listen. Our roots are common. We are brothers with one purpose, and that is, to return this island to its past well-being. So much was lost in slaving for others. We must now work for ourselves. We'll make the heavens dwell amidst us. The sweet dew of the Bermudas will saturate the earth again, and vineyards will be heavy with grapes, and palms and cedars will wave in the winds from the sea.
CALIBAN: We will till the land and bring rivers from the hills; the grain will stand tall in the fields and fresh water smile in our pitchers. Hark, I hear a storm getting up; it's Sycorax' soul passing above us, making its way back to Setebos. Ariel, my mother leaves me.
ARIEL: Grieve not for her, Caribima.

>   Her time was up. Come, you must
>   send off her soul with due honour.
> CALIBAN: I must
>   perform my mother's funeral rites. Fire must
>   burn to purify her soul and carry only
>   the indestructible essence to Setebos.
> ARIEL: Festivities befitting her status,
>   and desired by her will be performed.
>   Hark! Listen to the voices! The island
>   is alive. Can you hear them calling our
>   names? Come, Caliban – no, Caribima,
>   it's time the Caribs came together
>   as one nation of the Bermudas.

CALIBAN & ARIEL exeunt. Sounds of fire burning and drumbeats suggest cremation of SYCORAX. Soon the sound of festivities takes over. People are heard competing in games and sports. The sounds fade; light dawns and birds are heard twittering.

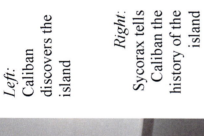

Left:
Caliban discovers the island

Right: Sycorax tells Caliban the history of the island

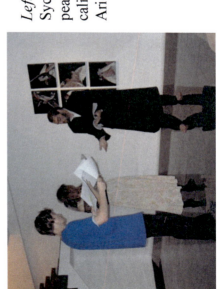

Left: Sycorax makes peace between caliban and Ariel

Right: Mapachitl, Wutki and Atuki

Left:
Mapachitl, Caliban, Tsilah

Right: Tsilah convinces Caliban of her love

Below: the masked celebration for the wedding of Caliban and Tsilah (*left*). The gods also join them (*right*)

Act III

Scene i

Two men enter singing. They are carrying spades and buckets. They have been working in the fields and have just harvested grapes. While singing they take out a bottle of wine, bread and fruit from their buckets. They are rough and hearty. All through their conversation, they express themselves in guffaws and thigh-and-back slapping much to substantiate their vocabulary. Many times, they falter in singing, as they can't remember the words.

>A paradise in ocean, this island is our haven.

>Five years we tilled the land,
>dug deep for wells and trees,
>grew forests for birds and beasts.
>Food and fish in plenty now.

>A paradise in ocean, this island is our haven.

>Vineyards stretch far and wide. Grapes
>are crushed and wine is drunk; gods made
>tipsy to bless us more. Smile, smile, smile.

>A paradise in ocean, this island is our haven.

>No invaders can rule us now; they can come
>and they can go, but not stay, and will do
>as they are told. They can buy our grapes,
>fruit and grain, take our wares away,
>and that's all we'll let them do for us.

>A paradise in ocean, this island is our haven.

> Freedom is our staple and work our virtue.
> No lords stamp on these grounds, only gods
> and people breath the air of this land.
>
> A paradise in ocean, this island is our haven.

They flop down, laughing and drinking and eating.

ATUKI: Hey-ho. What do you say? Our singing good for tomorrow?
WUTKI: Yea, methinks it is. Enough for today. My lungs are bursting for lack of liquid, Liberation Day or not. How long are we going to go on with these big celebrations of the end of slavery?
ATUKI: It gets tiring. Long speeches from Caribima: how many wells have been dug, and how many trees and vineyards – twenty, thirty? – planted since last year.
WUTKI: And Olokum will talk of tribal solidarity and unity in the face of foreign invasion of our island; and how sea traffic is increasing, with more ships sailing past our coast.
ATUKI: And that will start the next topic of…
TOGETHER: Fortifications! No long-long-stay anchoring on our shores!
ATUKI: I can't see any problem. We can fix an anchoring toll, which can be some ware from their country. But Caribima and Olokum are so set on not letting the ships stop here.
WUTKI: They can do what they like, but they shouldn't make the Liberation Day a long tedious business. We hear the same thing every year.
ATUKI: But not the songs, they are new. And damn me if I can remember the damn words.
WUTKI: Upon my soul, they are difficult. Not like simple songs of drink and women.
ATUKI: And food. Hey, man, we have drink and food, but no woman. Why not?

WUTKI: *(thinks)* I can't think why not. Now, when was it I last lay down with a woman?
ATUKI: I can't either. *(Counting)* I make only four. You?
WUTKI: Only three? Can you remember who she was?
ATUKI: *(aghast)* No, I can't? But does one have to?
WUTKI No, not really. But it would be fun, if we had a woman more often, the same perhaps, do you agree?
ATUKI: Oh, yes. At least one between us. We don't need two, do we?
WUTKI: No, it can be sometimes you, and sometimes me.
ATUKI: Yea, good, and she can cook for both of us.
WUTKI: What about children? We can have the same children, can't we?
ATUKI: Oh, we can. *(Whispers)* It's not the children, I'm thinking of... *(gestures)*. Ohooo. What do you say?
WUTKI: Yea, go ahead. Hey, man, where do we find this woman?
ATUKI: You blind? The land is steaming with lasses. It's just that we've been working too hard and not having enough sex.
WUTKI: True, true, now that you mention it. I didn't give it enough thought before.
ATUKI: Well, I'm not too good at thinking.
WUTKI: We should tell Caribima. Maybe he can find us a woman.
ATUKI: What can he do? He hasn't one himself.
WUTKI: Then, what about Olokum? He's our chief, he'll do it?
ATUKI: Does he know anything about women? Come to think of it, none of us seem to know what it is to sleep with a woman.

MAPACHITL enters. He looks like a troublemaker, and joins them with some evil intention.

MAPACHITL: How goes the time, mates? *(Mocking Caribima's tone)* What! drinking and lounging? Not working? *(In his own voice)* So, what's up?

WUTKI: Nothing really. Have some wine.
ATUKI: Wutki, should we tell Mapachitl what we were thinking?
WUTKI: Yes, yes, that would be good. You tell him.
ATUKI: No, you say it better. You tell him.
MAPACHITL: Shall I tell you what you were thinking?
TOGETHER: (*Amazed*) You could!!
MAPACHITL: Let me try. Now, first you were thinking about the National Day tomorrow, and what a bore it is. All those speeches you will have to listen to, and the songs you will have to sing when the words are far too difficult to learn.
WUTKI: Oh, you know everything! *(To ATUKI)* Isn't he clever?
ATUKI: We were talking, weren't we? *(To MAPACHITL)* You must have overheard us?
WUTKI: No, he didn't. He knows what we are thinking. Now, go on, Mapachitl, I like it when someone can tell me what I am thinking.
MAPACHITL: *(slowly)* First, you thought there was too much work. Always digging, sowing, harvesting, stacking, and that it's too tiring. Am I right?
WUTKI: Oh, you are like fantastic. Isn't he?
ATUKI: Yes, yes, he is. I did think that.
MAPACHITL: Then you thought of here *(pointing to the crotch*) and said, but not enough for here. No woman to dig into, you know what I mean.
ATUKI: That's right, I certainly thought that.
MAPACHITL: Then, you thought of asking Caribima, right?
TOGETHER: Yes, a little.
MAPACHITL: I think they are good thoughts.
WUTKI: You do?
ATUKI: He said he did.
MAPACHITL: Because I think the same.

ALL clap hands in a touché manner.

Truly, we never stop. Caribima goes on, from one

project to another: from growing grain (*the others keep a count on their fingers, nodding heads*) to planting trees to digging wells to storing food – have I forgotten anything *(stops)*?

WUTKI: And hunting.

ATUKI: And learning songs – difficult words – for the anniversary festival – every year, year after year.

MAPACHITL: Yes, that's a point and nothing for here – *(pointing again to the crotch)*. Not right, is it?

W & A: No, it isn't./ We were saying that ourselves.

MAPACHITL: So, we should tell Caribima what we think.

W & A: Not sure, if we should./ We did think of it, but then didn't./ Hey, maybe, we should.

MAPACHITL: One thing you have to remember is that Caribima is just one of us, he has no reason to lord it over you. So, let's work out what you say to him.

W & A: *(panic-stricken)* But you'll come with us?

MAPACHITL: Yes, I will, but it's you who have to speak up. I'll help you. Okay, now. Let's start. One, too much work. You are treated like beasts of burden; made to work for long hours like slaves: plain slavery on a free island. Two, your body is being wasted in digging with spades rather than with your cocks. You must stress that (*O, we will, we will, we feel that here*). Three, one five-year plan was all right, but to go into another without a rest, is plain slavery. But you would happily be a slave, if there was also something else to do – you know what I mean. So, the conclusion is that you want a woman.

W & A: Oh, yes, / one for the two of us.

MAPACHITL: You are ready to make it economical.

WUTKI: But you see the problem is that Caribima himself does not have a woman, does he?

ATUKI: That's his problem. Why should we have to follow his example?

MAPACHITL: The question is: will a woman have him? Not with that ugly face he has? You must have noticed.

W & A: No, we didn't./ You are right. /That must be the

reason.
MAPACHITL: And look at you two – good-looking, young and strong. There should be a stampede among women to get you.
WUTKI: You think so? I never thought I was good-looking.
ATUKI: Me too. We can't wait any longer. You have made us see the truth.
MAPACHITL: Well, you need time to think of yourself, and there isn't any.
W & A: *(angry)* Caribima has cheated us for too long. We will tell Olokum what we think. And by Setebos, he will hear us, loud and full. The gods have not sent you to us for nothing. Let's go to him, now. We are angry. Mapachitl, lead us.
MAPACHITL: This way then, good folks.

ALL exeunt.

Scene ii

OLOKUM (previously ARIEL) & TSILAH enter.

TSILAH: Brother, what is it you want to tell me? And so urgent that you couldn't wait until this evening?
OLOKUM: It is something you must have time to think about. Rushed matters haste the mind without reason.
TSILAH: Well?
OLOKUM: Caribima. You think him a good man?
TSILAH: Yes, he is hardworking, though a little hard on workers; gentle yet short in manner; goodhearted but not always given to compassion; all in all, yes, I would say he is a man of honour and loyalty.
OLOKUM: Good enough to be loved?
TSILAH: Oh, yes, it would depend on how he approaches the woman.

OLOKUM: Know of a young lass who would fancy him?
TSILAH: Let me think. Now, there's Emanjah,
balanced and even-tempered, she likes
honourable men, but not those who regard
work as honour, so she won't do; then,
there is Urzuli, full of fancy and flight,
and adores men who laugh and chatter; and
though Caribima is good company,
he is not much fun to be with; so she won't
do. Ah, Agweta, bubbly and giggly like
the high tide, she dreams of men strong
and striding, but also fears them, and
Caribima, though he would come tops in
strength, we all know, falls short on
the patience side. Now, Itaba, so much
like the goddess she is named after,
tolerates all shortcomings in men,
but wants to control them absolutely.
Hmm. A bit on the tyrannical side, I
would say. No, I wouldn't wish her on poor
Caribima. Who else? I'm afraid, the list
has run out of potential women
for him. Why do you ask?
OLOKUM: Because the time
for Caribima's nuptials is close;
in fact, very soon.
TSILAH: How soon?
OLOKUM: Tomorrow,
on the National Day. Arrangements
have to be made.
TSILAH: Why so rushed, brother?
OLOKUM: The stars are favourable, the occasion
auspicious.
TSILAH: For whom?
OLOKUM: For the tribe? Nuptials
are not only for the young. Does it
make sense? To you?
TSILAH: Brother, what's on your mind? Why ask

me so pointedly?
ARIEL: Tsilah, would you
   think of Caribima as your partner?
TSILAH: I see,
   I was led on. Not very honourable, brother.
OLOKUM: How do you like your man, sister? Same as
   your friends, or differently?
TSILAH: I like a good-looking man, and Caribima
   is not. Short and true is my answer, Olokum.
OLOKUM: That's vanity over goodness. Outer
   appearances are like waters by the shore;
   you cannot anchor in them.
TSILAH: Anchorage
   is not an everyday affair. Harbours
   are a once-in-a-life time need, but the tide
   in its ebb and flow is a daily delight,
   and the moon waxing or waning. Goodness
   for body and mind. The eye must feast,
   must hold hands with beauty, if a wholeness
   is to be effected. I speak from the heart
   and head both, brother. Can you understand
   a woman's need?
OLOKUM: Sister, it is not up
   to me to understand individuals.
   My vision is fixed on timeless cycles
   of destruction and creation.
TSILAH: Am I
   to cry or laugh at your words, Olokum?
OLOKUM: Tsilah, take heart, sister. What seems so bad
   is not always so. I am bound by my word
   and cannot tell you what I know. But let
   this suffice for the woman's heart, that your
   desire will not be squashed. Caribima
   is not what he looks; a change in looks would
   follow a change of heart.
TSILAH   It cannot be.
   We are unique and remain for one life
   the way we were born. Like the stars

on the heavenly fabric, we shine in our
own uniqueness, changing would
effect distortion. No, brother, Caribima
is not for me, though I hate him not.
OLOKUM: Alas, your words cannot alter what fates
already decreed for you at your birth.
TSILAH: Why at my birth? And who dared do it?
OLOKUM: Shaman Atekoshang. Just before her death,
she prophesied that the next birth in our
our family would be of a girl, who would be
wedded to Caribima.
TSILAH: By Setebos, I shall defy her decree.
OLOKUM: By Setebos himself, you were betrothed
to Caribima. Oh, sister, trust the tribal
ways; there is a reward for every deed.
Believe me. Happiness will not elude you.
TSILAH: It already has. Tribe or fates, I am
the sacrifice you make to them.
OLOKUM: O, sister,
Trust me, and you will not....Look, some people.

TSILAH is disheartened, and sits down under the tree. The three men enter. W & A are nervous but trying to be brave, whispering and nudging MAPACHITL, who is full of bravado and righteous rebellion.

Act IV

Scene i

Throughout the scene the shifts in relationship take place between people, heightening the tension in the plot. From being silent and unhappy earlier in the scene, TSILAH changes as she reacts strongly to MAPACHITL.

OLOKUM: Is something the matter? Wutki? Atuki?
W & A: No, no, there isn't./ We were coming to wish you a good day/ yes, yes, a good day, and wanted to ask/ about tomorrow's programme./ You know, the National Day./ Isn't that right Mapachitl?
MAPACHITL: Cowards. How dare you ask me to come with you, and then back down?
W & A: No, no, please go ahead/, tell Olokum./ Olokum, Mapachitl will tell you what we want to say.
OLOKUM: I am baffled.
W&A: Go, ahead, Mapachitl./ We apologise.
MAPACHITL: That's better. Now, Olokum, these good folks have something to say.
OLOKUM: Right, let me hear.
MAPACHITL: In fact, Wutki and Atuki have two complaints. Their first complaint is: there is too much work; they have to do too much work.
OLOKUM: No more than all of us.
MAPACHITL: Yes, but they have less leisure than some of you. They are at work constantly, slave-driven from one job to the next. As soon as they finish one they are given another. *(To W&A)* Isn't that so?
W & A: Oh, very much, very much.
OLOKUM: By whom?
MAPACHITL: By Caribima, who else? He is in charge of agricultural projects, isn't he? As labourers, these

people never have any rest.
W&A: That's right, no rest./ And no other involvement.
MAPACHITL: In other words, no physical pleasures. They can't remember when they last slept with a woman.
W & A: Absolutely true./ Not even one between us.
OLOKUM: Neither does Caribima.
MAPACHITL: Yes, but you have plans for him, not for them.
OLOKUM: They are free to look for their mates. There is no restriction on them.
MAPACHITL: Oh, yes, there is restriction on them, the beasts of burden that they are.
OLOKUM: Stop there, Mapachitl. You are crossing all limits.
MAPACHITL: It's you who has crossed the limits by favouring an outsider. Explain why you refused me your sister when you were arranging to match her with that migrant?
TSILAH: O treacherous love! Brother, look at me, am I the last to know your plans for fixing me up with a man?
OLOKUM: There is no first or last. I had reasons to break the news slowly to you.
MAPACHITL: What's wrong with me? Am I not better looking than that ugly foreigner? Or am I not a native of this island? Answer me.
OLOKUM: There are reasons why I can't answer your accusations before tomorrow. But let me remind you that Caribima is not a migrant. He is as much of this island as you, me or Wutki and Atuki, and also Tsilah, for that matter.
MAPACHITL: Oh, I see, he's not a migrant, even though he comes from another land, has the blood of the invaders? Is that it?
OLOKUM: Everyone knows he was born on this island. You choose to forget it, Mapachitl.
MAPACHITL: And was his mother born here too? And what about his grandparents, and all the previous generations of the ancestors? Why do you treat him so

specially?

OLOKUM: Because Shaman Atekoshang accepted his mother as one of us, in fact more than one of us, as Sycorax was a shaman in her own right. She also bore a son to Chief Loco, and named him Caribima, the son of the Caribs, that's more than I can say for you.

MAPACHITL: If you can't see the difference between a pure native and a half breed, then you are no good to the people of this island.

CARIBIMA is heard calling 'Olokum', 'Olokum'.

OLOKUM: Here comes Caribima. Wutki & Atuki, you can address your work grievances to him directly. And Mapachitl, you can air your hostility to him.

CARIBIMA enters

Caribima, some complaints have been brought against you. Give Wutki and Atuki a hearing. Wutki, Atuki, go ahead.

W & A: Can Mapachitl speak for us?/ He knows what we said.

OLOKUM: No, you must learn to speak for yourself. If you want to change things, you must stand up for them.

MAPACHITL: Come on, boys, I will help you.

CARIBIMA: Keep out of it, Mapachitl. You will have your turn. Yes, Wutki, Atuki?

WUTKI: All right. Caribima, we think – that is, I and Atuki – that we have become beasts of burden.

ATUKI: Of course we like to see our island green and flourishing.

WUTKI: Yes, and flowers and fruit, trees and forests, but we feel too tired and....

ATUKI: And overworked. We do nothing else, but dig and till the earth, and go to sleep like the beasts of the forests.

CARIBIMA: So, what do you want?
WUTKI: Not such long hours of work.
ATUKI: We don't watch the sunset, or sing when the moon is up...
WUTKI: Or feel the sap running in our limbs...
ATUKI: At most we have our drink and then flop down...
WUTKI: And sleep without dreaming...
ATUKI: Next day it starts all over again.
CARIBIMA: All right, all right, I get the picture. I am not unaware of the problem, but we needed to finish the project by the National Day.
W & A: Oh, yes, yes, we know what you mean./ We also want to.
CARIBIMA: After that, the work hours will be reduced. You should have spoken before. If you don't speak up, you don't get what you want. Anything else?
MAPACHITL: Keep going, now's the time.
OLOKUM: And you keep out of it.
WUTKI: Even beasts mate and propagate their species.
ATUKI: But we don't.
CARIBIMA: And why not?
W & A: We don't know why not. Yes, I do know./ Because we follow your example./ We say, don't we, if Caribima doesn't have a woman, then who are we to have one?/ Correct, we do say that./ Now, if you set us an example, then we can use our sticks which Legba has put on us to beat our women with./ What else do we have dicks for, eh?
CARIBIMA: You are not tied down to me, Wutki and Atuki. We have different temperaments. You must do what you want, and leave me to mine.
W & A: But a lot is up to you. You must build us a community hut where we can meet girls and dance and sing./ The drink bar is bad for us./ It's no good for feeling human.
CARIBIMA: A good point. It will be put down in the next National Plan.
W & A: I hope sooner than that./ We don't want to be old

men before we have it.
CARIBIMA: Good point. It will be done sooner.
OLOKUM: Right, that settles the easier of the two grievances. Now, Caribima, Mapachitl here complains that you have no right to the island, as you are an immigrant, someone who will always remain an outsider. So, what do you say in your defence?
CARIBIMA: Mapachitl, what does it take for one to be of the island?
MAPACHITL: Ancestors.
CARIBIMA: How many generations?
MAPACHITL: As many as the mind can remember. You were born here but no one before you. Your mother was an immigrant, and that makes you one too.
CARIBIMA: Mapachitl, I have a feeling, reason won't get me anywhere with you. Tomorrow, at the Carnival, people can vote for or against me. Would that be satisfactory to you?
MAPACHITL: I don't like your tricks, Caliban *(emphasis)*. Let me tell you, I have found out everything about you.
CARIBIMA: Some of us outlive our past experiences, Mapachitl. I do not want to get entangled in your hostility towards me.
MAPACHITL: Some would see it as valid to any native claim.
CARIBIMA: See what?
MAPACHITL: Taking away our women, when we go without them.
TSILAH: *(Interrupting CARIBIMA as he is about to make the reply)* Enough, Mapachitl. You are crossing all limits. But if any reply has to be made to your malicious claim, I'll make it.
MAPACHITL: Tsilah, you keep out of it. It's nothing to do with you.
TSILAH: Oh, isn't it? I just happen to be one of the island women you are talking about. But of course, I have no right to speak on behalf of us or for myself.
MAPACHITL: It's something between men, between

Olokum, me and Caliban.
CARIBIMA: How does Olokum come into the picture, if you are attacking me for taking up with women of the island?
MAPACHITL: Because he is matching you with his sister.
CARIBIMA: Heavens! Me and Tsilah?
W & A: See, if only you weren't doing too much work, you would have found out what everybody else knows about you.
CARIBIMA: Olokum, is that true?
TSILAH: Yes, it is true. He was going to tell you, but he first had to ask me.
OLOKUM: Caribima, it's not me; the gods have decreed it.
MAPACHITL: Stop blaming the gods for your own failures. I will not let it happen. What will be left of this island, if all the women choose foreigners over the natives?
TSILAH: So, what are you going to do about it?
MAPACHITL: I will get the elders to stop this arrangement. It's not fair on the natives that the foreigners walk away with the best of our products.
TSILAH: You might as well forget about it, Mapachitl, because this 'product' will tell them that it prefers a foreigner to a native.
MAPACHITL: What you say is not important.
TSILAH: Oh, yes, it is. You will regret opening your mouth, when I tell them why Caribima – and not Caliban – will make a better partner for me, and for what sound reasons I choose him over you.
MAPACHITL: *(To CALIBIMA & OLOKUM)* I will see you both there.
TSILAH: *(barring his way)* You will first hear me out, so that you don't disgrace yourself before the elders.
MAPACHITL: All right. Tell me how is he better than me? Why would you choose him?
TSILAH: I choose Caribima over you, Mapachitl, because he is a better human being than you. While you are arrogant, he is humble, while you are an opportunist and a backbiter, he is loyal and compassionate; in nature,

you are jealous and dishonest. You may be good-looking, Mapachitl, but your heart is ugly. You misled these simple folks to air your own complaint.
According to the tradition of the Carib tribe, the girl has the final say in her match with a man. As a native you should know that. The reason Olokum could not tell Caribima earlier was because he had to tell me first. He considered my feelings in the matter important while all that time you were spreading spiteful rumours.

MAPACHITL: Olokum, is this final?

OLOKUM: Calm yourself, Mapachitl. Think coolly. Caribima cannot be thought of separately from us. The sooner you understand that, the better it is. The gods have decreed thus. In me all our ancestors speak. Tomorrow, Caribima and Tsilah will be wedded, not just ordinary nuptials, but ones with special significance for our island. What that is can be declared tomorrow. What gods decree cannot be undone by mortals.

Pause

Wutki and Atuki, tomorrow, you must look for your matches too; woo the lasses, go to their parents, convince them, and make your own happiness. As for your workload, you have spoken to Caribima. He will take your complaint seriously.

W & A: We will, we will. We must go now.

Exeunt

OLOKUM: And Mapachitl, envy and ill-will won't do you any good. I hope my words have spoken to you.

MAPACHITL: There is nothing left now.

OLOKUM: Yes, there is. At the Carnival tomorrow, new appointments for the next National Plan will be announced. There will be a change in the responsibilities. I will declare you as in-charge of irrigation projects. Caribima will be relieved of the office. And as for finding a lass for yourself, I am sure

there are women who are waiting for you.
MAPACHITL: Can't, not after what Tsilah has said about
me.
OLOKUM: Come, come, Mapachitl, not all women think
alike. Walk with me, I have more to tell.
CARIBIMA: *(rushing after him)* Stop, Olokum, by Setebos,
do not leave me in this confounded state.
TSILAH: Wait, Caribima, I will explain.
OLOKUM: Tsilah knows everything. Come, Mapachitl.

OLOKUM & MAPACHITL exeunt.

Scene ii

CARIBIMA: Why mock me, Tsilah? And now Olokum is gone.
O, for pity's sake, leave me alone.
TSILAH: Caribima, look at me, and say if
in these eyes, you see mockery making
faces at you?
CARIBIMA: But why would you want me,
Tsilah? No, no, it's not my fate to dream
of love. This ugly face, this savage body
cannot be the object of a woman's desire.
TSILAH: Did you not hear me tell Mapachitl that
I choose you over him?
CARIBIMA: Pity and charity make
poor handmaidens to Love. For a long time
I have lived in the shadow of the wilderness.
Why now rake up the ashes of burnt hopes
and shrunken emotions?
TSILAH: Your perception is faulty;
it is blind to good intentions.
CARIBIMA: That's it.
'Good intentions' are acts of charity
for the down and out. No, thanks, sister,
for your bravado in consorting with
the ugly and the savage.
TSILAH: O, dear heart,

you are neither, not with a heart as clear
as the summer sky, as vast as the ocean's
reach and as true as the coast of this island.
CARIBIMA: Enough, enough, let me not hear what I
cannot keep as my own.
TSILAH: O Legba,
let shafts of sunlight dispel his blindness,
and make him see the false from the true.
I admit I too was blind like you, but then
I saw the truth. How can I now make you
see my honesty?

No Answer.

Or is it that you
don't like women?
CARIBIMA: I didn't say that. *(Pause)* Often I
have felt the need for someone close, to whom
I could bare my soul, but I am too afraid
to approach a woman, for the fear of being
laughed at to my face — ugly and repulsive
to tender eyes. Hesitation has become
second nature to me. Beggars cannot
be choosers, Tsilah.
TSILAH: And you think I am
laughing at you now? Did you not hear me
tell Mapachitl why I like you better
than him? Should that not settle it for ever?
CARIBIMA: O, Setebos, god of the brave Patagonians,
make me not a prey to illusions. Let hope
not play tricks on me. O, god of beauty,
let me remain forgotten by roving hearts. *(Rushes behind the tree).*
TSILAH: O, foolish heart that does not feel, and eyes
that cannot see, then Coatrischie, O Great
Goddess, let my words be carried by wind
and storm and rent the very heavens:
(very loud) Tsilah loves Caribima. *(Pause, echo, softer now)* O Caribima, I love you because

you are like this island, earthy and real,
and always there. I love you because you
are like the ocean itself. In you is the ebb
and flow of our hopes and aspirations;
like the opaque sea that reflects these lovely
hills and forests, and makes us the envy of
passers-by, in your honesty this island
finds its true meaning. *(Pause)* Shall I go on?
Too long is the list of reasons of love.
O Caribima, come out and tell me
that you believe me.

Silence.

                          I have known you as long
as I have my brother. From birth we were
meant to be wed. Your mother told Olokum
that the Island Soul had forecast our union;
I was angry when he told me, but then
I understood. Now that the curtain of
ignorance is lifted, shall we celebrate?

Silence

    O Baron Samedi, God of magic, lift the spell
on Caribima, and let the truth dazzle him.

CARIBIMA emerges. He is changed into a good-looking man; but he remains unaware of it. TSILAH falls on her knees in wonder and awe at his looks.

    Ochumare, O goddess, behold your rainbow
over the firmament. Gone are the storm
and lightning that rent the skies. Behold
the return of Caribima to his pristine visage.
CARIBIMA: *(rushing to her)* Tsilah, are you delirious?
    What are these words? What illusions haunt
your face? Suspend all talk of my own; let me
live with it as it is. Mock me no further

(hesitant) if you love me.
TSILAH: *(still in excitement)* O Olokum, you were so right, my love has changed Caribima.
CARIBIMA: I am still the same, Tsilah. Look, look at me, do I look different?
TSILAH: *(breathless)* Oh yes, oh yes, you do; the gods too see a different Caribima.
CARIBIMA: You are not well, Tsilah. I'll take you to the healer, he'll give you a herb potion.
TSILAH: It's you who needs a potion, to open your eyes to see yourself. O, but how can that be? How can the seer see himself? O impossible man, give in, and let my eyes be a mirror to your sight. Mirror! Reflection! O Aida Wedo, why did I not think of your fresh waters? Come, come with me, Caribima, to the lake, where in the crystal water, the goddess of pure vision will reveal the truth of your visage, and your eyes can see what I see now. And Caliban will then see Caribima, Then beauty will hold hands with love, and Tsilah will never part from Caribima. The gods will descend to earth to bless us.

Exeunt.

Act V

Scene i

Sound of festivities. The National Day is being celebrated with a Carnival in full swing. In elaborate masks, people jostle and dance and sing. There is an atmosphere of abandonment and merry-making.

A sound of music formally announcing the opening of the Carnival. Everyone stops and waits. OLOKUM enters on a float. He wears the mask of GOD OLOKUM, who is the hermaphrodite god of the ocean depths. OLOKUM gets out of the float and performs the oblations to LEGBA, God of the Sun.

> Legba, God of the Sun, I bring oblations
> to you for rising every day in the great vault;
> there, I see you play with Ochu, the Moon-Goddess,
> who consorts with the Night. How you
> throw your crimson mantle on her pale face
> and allure her to the eastern sky. Look
> how your rival slinks away, wounded by
> your thousand shafts. O Gods of the heavenly
> spheres, we celebrate your union
> with nuptials of us mortals upon earth.
> Ochu, come with your luminous
> light, and Legba, bring dazzling brightness
> to protect us from the evil spirits
> that lie in wait to lay waste such godly
> rituals. O divine couple, be our guests
> at the nuptials of Caribima and Tsilah,
> mere reflections of your celestial light.
> O Fox-God, Aguara, you too we invite
> to see how the Caribs transplant the tree

you stole for them with your adoring
cunning. Come, be with us, and keep the enemy
away. Hark! A terrible noise fills the air,
the ocean heaves, a tempest is abroad,
the evil spirits are in chase. Ahoy, Guards,
(two guards rush in) quick, haste, move, the enemy
is at the gate, take up your positions,
do not let them slip past, beware of their
cunning, their masks of goodness.

GUARD I: Fear not, we know their craft too well...

GUARD II: ...and have dealt fatal blows to them before. Greed and pillage marks them out clearly.

OLOKUM: Be vigilant, make no allowance.
They lay waste whatever comes their way.
So, hold them at bay from desecration.
The nuptials must take place without fail.
I shall return to the bride and the groom,
and make sure no shadow falls on them. *(Exit)*

GUARD I: Hark! I hear their pattering feet close.

GUARD II: There they come, the Diablesse, the
dead virgins jealous of the bride. Look,
there, behind them trots Agaman Nibo,
the Goddess of the Dead. She leads them
by the hand, a skull garland jingling
from her round hip.

GUARD I: See further behind, how
cunning Christalline pushes forward, bringing
storms and all the evils of the sea to harm
and disrupt the harmony here.

GUARD II: Quick, move,
waylay them with speed.

GUARD I: Like a hurricane they come.

Music of discordant sounds. Three masked figures enter. One is the Diablesse; she has a multiple mask of the dead virgins, and a belt of skulls hangs from her hip. She is followed by Baron Samedi; he is the father of the gods of cemeteries. Following him is Christalline, the Evil Sea Goddess. They wear masks appropriate to their characteristics. Their entry is marked by threatening and destructive sounds. The Guards waylay them, evoking the power of the gods and issuing loud war cries.

GUARD I: *(war cries)* Come, God Agoun, rain fire on our enemies;
GUARD II: *(louder)* Come with spells of war and destruction.
GUARD I & II: Make us vanquish the evil before us.

Shouts of attack increase. The enemy is taken head on with loud utterances. 'Here, take this one,' & 'this one', 'out of my way' etc. A fierce fight breaks out; both sides engage in offensive and defensive skills. Eventually, the intruders are thrown down, defeated and forced to exit. The GUARDS are exhilarated by their victory. A show of victory is made with the announcement that the place is clear for the nuptials.

GUARD I: They've gone. Peace reigns again. The birds are astir.
    Listen to their twitter. Olokum, come,
    the path is clear and all is harmony now.
GUARD II: Bring the bride and the groom. The nuptials can begin. The gods await your call to them.

Music of the spheres is heard. OLOKUM appears, followed by Tsilah and Caliban as Ochu, the Moon Goddess, and as Legba, the Sun God.

OLOKUM: O Gods of the Bermudas, come and grace
    the nuptials of the Caribs. The hills have
    shed their dark visage and a rainbow arches
    above the dew-drenched island. Listen
    to the betrothed here, they call on you
    to partake in the ritual of their union.

As TSILAH and CALIBAN invoke the various gods – Aida Wedo, the goddess of the rainbow and fresh water, Oshun, goddess of love and fertility, Azacca, god of agriculture and Eleggua, the messenger god, healer, magician and the owner of roads and opportunities, without whom no ceremonies can take place. The gods enter wearing their appropriate masks and carrying the objects which represent them. They are welcomed with great gusto and loud music.

TSILAH: Come Aido Wedo, goddess of the rainbow
and fresh water, stretch your bow over
our new abode, drape the seven-coloured
garland around us; sprinkle your heavenly
waters on us and free us of disease,
so that what springs from us is pure and good.

AIDO WEDO enters. She is welcomed with cheers.

I call you too, Oshun, shower your sweet love
on us mortals and make us fertile with
new life. Come and be with us, warm our
home and hearth with destiny unmatched.
We sing your praises, O consort of Damballa,
whose springs and rivers change into live
snakes that dig their way deep into the earth.

OSHUN enters.

CALIBAN: Hear me, God Azacca, honour us with your
presence. Bring us your plough and spade,
our earth awaits your strength; make our fields
ripe with grain and hay and dot the land
with palms and dates everywhere. O lord
of iron limbs, make us dig deep to furrow
the soil, our ancestral island for seed new.

God AZACCA enters.

Now, all the gods are assembled, except
the one without whom we cannot begin.
Eleggua, the guardian god of all ceremonies,
come and preside over the wedding of Tsilah
and me. Give us your approval and dwell
with us. You, the healer, the protector, all-knower
of roads, put us on the right path through
life and death. Come, Eleggua, the tribe
of the Caribs awaits your presence now
to set us on the path of prosperity.

God ELEGGUA enters. Cheers and excitement. The nuptials begin amidst music and singing. The gods bless the newly-weds and join in the dancing. OLOKUM goes around, talking and chatting with people. He checks out with the masked figures who are behind the masks.

OLOKUM: *(to Goddess OSHUN)* Is that Wutki? *(WUTKI: Yes, I am)* How goes it?
OSHUN/WUTKI: Never thought it could be so much fun.
OLOKUM: With a woman?
OSHUN/WUTKI: Only! to think how much I missed out all this years!
OLOKUM: Never mind the past, Wutki. It's what's now that matters.
OSHUN/WUTKI: Couldn't agree more. Same with Atuki, see over there, how happy he looks, his mask bobbing up and down, like a see-saw.
OLOKUM: He does. *(Hails goddess AIDO WEDO)* Atuki, how's life?
WEDO/ATUKI: *(continues with the movement)* Couldn't be better. I never want to stop. Oh, to be drunk on the sweet waters of Oshun. I say, Olokum, you need to try it some time.
OLOKOM: *(laughs, patting him)* Some of us can't manage it, dear Atuki. *(Looks around)* Which one is Mapachitl?
WEDO/ATUKI: That one, over there. He's had such a

scoop, you won't find a happier man.
OLOKUM: *(taps god ZAKA on the shoulder)* Hey there, are you the happiest man?
ZAKA/MAPACHITL: I am, I am, Olokum. You've changed my life. Even the gods don't give so much. *(OLOKUM puts a finger on his lips, pointing to the gods, MAPACHITL drops his voice to a whisper.)* Not only the headship of the agriculture ministry but a woman to go with it!
OLOKUM: I saw you chatting up Erzuli. Is it working out?
ZAKA/MAPACHITL: Ask her, there she is *(points to god ELEGGUA)* O Olokum, she is more divine than Oshun herself *(OLOKUM shushes him again).* Find out for yourself. *(Gives him a push towards the masked figure of Oshun).*
OLOKUM: *(putting his hand on her shoulder)* Erzuli *(the figure lifts the mask, showing him her face. OLOKUM is startled)* Sycorax, you here?
OSHUN/SYCORAX: Yes, Olokum. How could I not be? It's not every day one's son gets married.
OLOKUM: But how, how can you from the other world?
SYCORAX: If the gods can, Olokum, so can spirits, especially if they are good ones. Trust me, I am all right. *(Looks at the wedded couple)* How different Caribima looks. You had some struggle there, didn't you, Olokum?
OLOKUM: Yes, until Tsilah knew the truth about Caribima, she was reluctant.
SYCORAX: And now look what love can do. They look happy together. *(Pause)* And you, Olokum, how goes it with you?
OLOKUM: It goes well, Sycorax, but you know what happens to people like me.
SYCORAX: Some time to go yet, Olokum. You are still young.
OLOKUM: A bit lonely though. And what has youth to do with it when you are a living soul. Sycorax, what is it like out there?

SYCORAX: Lonely as you say, but one is freer. Time and
space are not restricted. Alas! Why do you ask?
OLOKUM: Last night I had a dream. *(Pause)* Sycorax, my
time is up. *(SYCORAX tries to interrupt him)* No, listen
to me, I must tell someone. My end is near. I have
chosen Tsilah and Caribima's child as the next vessel
for the Island Soul.
SYCORAX: *(distressed)* Don't, Olokum, it's too soon.
OLOKUM: These five years have been difficult. It's been
hard putting the island back on its feet after the
departure of Prospero. It was a big job, and it took a lot
out of me. We are over it now. The island is
prosperous and the people have a sense of belonging to
this place. But national memories are always short.
Except Caliban and me, no one knows what it was like
under the invaders. They lived a passive life, while we
both were yoked in slavery. Caribima has a new life
before him, but I belong to the past. There's nothing
here for me. I have transferred my responsibilities to
the new blood. It's time I do the same to my soul too.
It's the same what you did, Sycorax, you should
understand that *(he turns to her and finds he's talking to
no one. He looks around and sees the figure is dancing
with Mapachitl).* Sycorax *(he calls again. The figure
doesn't respond).* Was she not here? Is my mind
feverish? *(He turns to look at Tsilah and Caribima.
They are laughing and and dancing. They wave to him,
he waves back)* Ah! How happy they look. Something I
have accomplished. *(Moves towards them, then stops).*
Not now, I mustn't tell them now. There will be time
later. *(Looks out far into the horizon, lights begin to go
down)*

A dark and unknown journey ahead.
How long have I been on this island?
'A Paradise in Ocean' we sang today,
a different habitation from the desolate
place it was five years ago. Like alchemists

Caliban

we transformed the base life of slavery
into the gold of liberty and equality.
This has been my world, the place where I
was born and from where I will begin my
long journey. Would that I could recall my
beginning when this very earth nourished me,
the ocean cradled me, the winds sang me lullabies
and the forests became my playground.
(Tries to see something in the distance)
Is that me in the tree? Over there, huddled
in the cloven pine - no, no it's a cedar.
And there *(looks out)*, what's that? A ship making its
way to our harbour. *(Panics)* Ahoy! Someone, quick, stop
those sailors from landing on our island.

Lights go down.

Afterword

It's been over a decade and a half since two of the three plays in this collection were produced in Hungary and Romania. Although the memory of the experience is still there, it is not as sharp as that of the third play *Caliban* which was staged in Romania in 2011. Time has its ravages. Yet bringing out a collection does mean reviving old memories. *The III-Act Hamlet* had 22 roles (acted by 16 actors). In contrast *Shakespeare & Me* only 2! All contact with the actors has now been lost, yet I would like to thank all of them for making theatre history with these productions.

When *Caliban* was produced at The Blue Elephant Theatre in 2001, under the 'New Playwrights' scheme, it was good to sit back and enjoy the play being put together by others. The Romanian staging of *Caliban* being more recent is fresher in my memory. There was a good response from Shakespeare scholars from all over Eastern Europe who had arrived to celebrate the founding of a new Shakespeare symposium on gender.

Rani Drew

About the Author

I have been writing plays now for over 20 years. Feminist theatre made its appearance in the 1970s. By the 1980s there were a lot more plays written by women about women. The stage as a public platform was key to making women visible and audible. It was in 1988 that I committed myself to writing about women. In that one year alone, I wrote three plays and produced them myself. The first two, *The Oedipus Question* and *Sofia Tolstoy*, were staged in Cambridge; the third, *Women are Talking*, saw the stage lights in Shanghai. Since then, I have written many more plays, and have overtaken Shakespeare's total of thirty-six.

The plays are not only universal in theme but are set in diverse cultures and countries. This publication is the third in a series of collections of my plays.

PLAYS PRODUCED

Nov.,	2012	*King Prawns & Apple Pie*, Cambridge (UK)
June,	2012	*Three Riddle Plays* by Rabindranath Tagore, Cambridge
May,	2012	*The Great Wall of Adhamiya*, Cambridge
Nov.,	2011	*Caliban* (dramatised reading), Timişoara (Romania)
June,	2010	*Queen Victoria & the Maharaja of Punjab* (dramatised reading), Cambridge
Dec.,	2009	*The Man Behind Evolution*, Cambridge
July,	2009	*1859 – A Meeting of Poets & Scientists* (Darwin Festival, Cambridge)
Nov.,	2008	*Cleopatra* (in Punjabi) Amritsar (India)
Jan.,	2005	*Asian Galaxy*, Xinxiang (China)
Jan.,	2004	*Organ Donors*, Xinxiang
April,	2003	*Bradford's Burning*, Attic Theatre, London (UK)
June,	2002	*Eggs for Education*, Cambridge
June,	2001	*Caliban*, The Blue Elephant Theatre, London
May- Oct.,	1999	*Cleopatra*, Budapest (Hungary), Timişoara (Romania), Cambridge, Skopje (Macedonia), Granada (Spain)
May,	1998	*Diana & Others*, Budapest
Feb.,	1998	*Asia Calls*, Budapest
April,	1997	*Aranya Kozmetika*, Budapest
Dec.,	1996	*B for Beef: Buy British*, Budapest
Sept.,	1996	*Funeral Rites*, a radio play, Budapest
Dec.,	1995	*Shakespeare & Me*, Budapest, Debrecen (Hungary), Galaţi (Romania), Cambridge

April,	1995	*Sunday Mum'sday*, Budapest
April,	1994	*The Picture on the Wall*, Budapest & Pécs (Hungary)
April,	1993	*Totempole Supremo*, Budapest
May,	1992	*The III-Act Hamlet*, Budapest, Timişoara
May,	1990	*Pan Jinlian*, (*English adaptation of a Chinese Opera*), Shanghai (China)
June,	1989	*After Nora Left Home*, Shanghai
Dec.,	1988	*Women Are Talking*, Shanghai
July,	1988	*Sofia Tolstoy*, Cambridge
March,	1988	*The Oedipus Question*, Cambridge

PLAYS YET TO BE PRODUCED

2013	*The Unsung Heroine of the Double Helix*
2007	*Traffic Lights* (female trafficking & prostitution)
2007	*Cinderella on the Underground* (radio play, updating fairy tale)
2003	*The Cost of a Corpse* (the Kenyan bombings)
2002	*The Healers of Lekhapur* (witch-hunt in India)
2002	*Changing Platforms* (1960's immigrants at King's Cross)
1999	*Paradise Recovered* (environmental abuse of our planet)
1999	*The Streets of London* (radio play about racism)
1993	*Women on the Tower* (miners' wives' against UK pit closures in 1984)
1990	*Sati 1990* (India, women & socialism, 1989)
1990	*The Odyssey of Zhang Hui* (radio play, Chinese women)
1989	*The Play that Never Got Done* (play about Tiananmen that could not be staged in China)
1988	*Men's Decisions: Women's Choices* (Chinese women). Production denied in China

OTHER PUBLICATIONS BY THE AUTHOR

Three Plays: The Oedipal Question
             Sophia Tolstoy
             Women are Talking
The Making of a Chinese Play
Celestial Seductions (poetry)
Around the World in Twelve Stories
             (fiction), Skrev Press
Cleopatra & Asia Calls (plays)
Stories of All Ages (fiction)
Asian Galaxy (play)
Medea & Other Poems (poetry)
Glimpses of the World (poetry & fiction)
Plays-1, Chinese Women's Long March to Tiananmen
Plays-2, Science & Space
The Dog's Tale: a Life in the Buda Hills
             (novel), Whytetracks, Copenhagen, Denmark